ESSENTIAL

FRENCH

STYLE

ESSENTIAL
FRENCH
STYLE

JILL VISSER

WARD LOCK

To Owen and Nia

A WARD LOCK BOOK

First published in the UK 1995
by Ward Lock
Wellington House
125 Strand
LONDON
WC2R0BB

A Cassell Imprint

First paperback edition 1998

Distributed in the United States by Sterling Publishing Co., Inc. 387 Park Avenue South, New York, NY 10016-8810

A British Library Cataloguing in Publication Data block for this book may be obtained from the British Library

ISBN 0-7063-7746-X

Designed by Nick Clark
Illustrations by Jane Hughes
Printed and bound in Spain by Bookprint S.L.
Front cover photograph:
Camera Press/Bo Appeltofft
Back cover photograph:
Robert Harding Picture Library/ Nadia Mackenzie

CONTENTS

$\mathcal{I}$NTRODUCTION

ASK A FEW PEOPLE TO CONJURE UP A PICTURE of a typical French interior and chances are their descriptions will fall roughly into one of two categories: an elegant living room with formal, even ornate chairs, smart curtains, gilt-framed pictures and a mirror, or a rustic farmhouse with rough walls, a large cupboard – possibly painted, simple cotton fabrics, and a clutch of country chairs around a rustic dining table.

Yet, if you open any current French magazine, the pictures tell a completely different story – page after page of sleek, sparsely furnished, immaculately accessorized homes. Of course, in reality the variations on a French interior are much greater than the pigeonholes we slot them into and, as in any study of style, we end up pinpointing the best and/or most well-documented ingredients. But we can identify some common factors: solid floors, at least one impressive piece of furniture, a functional kitchen plus table, a spacious dining table and an admirable mirror. It is also true to say that links with the past are strong throughout the land and even the most contemporary atelier or apartment is likely to include a collection of well-loved, aged (though not necessarily valuable) pieces.

When it comes to our perception of French homes, the same adjectives crop up time and time again – stylish, comfortable, food/family orientated and chic. France to most is a nation of style gurus who enjoy their food and their homes.

This recognition of the French as style connoisseurs goes way back in time and as a race they have always exercised a great influence on international interior fashions. Many furnishing styles have been retained and enjoyed not only in France but the world over, occasionally in their original form, but more often adapted to suit a new generation's tastes and lifestyles.

The Empire-style bed is a case in point. A popular model at present in many retail outlets, it is a derivation of an early 19th-century French design. Then it was heavily canopied, bolstered and

Brightly coloured damasks are hallmarks of France, particularly of the Régence period. This striking collection shows rich ruby and taupe damasks with exotic forest scenes, which are reproductions of cloth as it would have been in the time of Louis XV.

counterpaned; now it is dressed in a duvet and teamed with lace-edged, machine-washable linen. But, this aside, the shape is basically the same.

On the whole, furnishings that we recognize as being of French origin today are more likely to stem from designs of the latter part of the 17th century and later.

BAROQUE (LOUIS XIV 1643–1715)

Interiors in the 17th century were extraordinarily theatrical. Featuring heavily carved furniture, tapestries and silk brocades, frescoed walls, shimmering chandeliers, gilded wood and cherubs, this extravagant mix was one of magnificent splendour. Louis XIV who adopted this look at the Palace of Versailles became known as the Sun King.

In more modest residences, illusion tricks like *trompe l'oeil* or fake marble columns were much in vogue. Although in its entirety, this style is too extreme to work in the average home of today, elements can create stunning dramatic overtones, especially in dining rooms. Cherub stencils, gilt mirrors and candlesticks, particularly in distressed condition, have been favourite themes in home products.

REGENCE (C1700–1725)

The following era, Régence, between the reigns of Louis XIV and Louis XV, was also one of grandeur. Influences from the Far East at this time meant a fashion for anything oriental – at first imported, but later when sources dwindled, made in France. Craftsmen mimicked the lustrous varnished finishes of these pieces and cabinets and console tables were showy and richly decorated. Chinoiserie became a popular interior look, often with whole rooms given the Chinese treatment.

ROCOCO (LOUIS XV C1730–1760)

It is perhaps the rococo period, around 45 years later in the middle chunk of Louis XV's reign, that is identifiably French to most people. With an emphasis on comfort, chairs were rounded, legs were curvy and details were of swirling carved forms. Wood was frequently gilded and all aspects of nature – shells, waves, fish, serpents, rocks and flowers – were common in relief, inlay or painted decoration on sofa and chair frames. Motifs depicting any enjoyable activity – the country, lovemaking, music, and even humour – were widely used too. Colours were bright and fabrics were rich, velvets and damasks being common upholstery fabrics.

The whole look was exaggerated and flamboyant but elements of it are much in evidence today. The fact that there was a revival of this style in the first half of the 19th century, coupled with ongoing interest in the Victorian period, accounts for a recent proliferation of rococo detail in home accessories, especially ornate mirrors and picture frames.

The Bergère or upholstered chair conceived a few decades earlier became popular. Some versions had space under the arms, others were upholstered but both had the same basic structure

– a stretcher-free wood-framed seat with arms set back to prevent crinolines being crushed. This armchair remains a favourite in many French homes to this day, with the style being accessible as it is still manufactured by several companies today. Originally upholstered in velvet, damask or tapestry, contemporary reproductions are more likely to feature woven cotton textiles.

What might be described today as a typical French wallpaper also has its origins in the latter part of the 18th century. Designs were influenced by the work of Flemish painters and tended to be delicate and light. By the mid-19th century, this concept had further developed into more flamboyant represen-tations with all-over patterns in a larger scale on a pale background, not unlike the chintzy florals that one would have assumed to be of British origin.

The imitation of textiles, which had started in the early days with straightforward copies of silk, velvet and tapestry providing a cheaper and easier way of covering walls than the real thing, were more ambitious by the end of the century. Designs mimicking pleats, drapes and folds of fabrics in three dimensions were so convincing that it was often difficult to distinguish them from the real thing. Even embroidered net and a buttoned upholstery effect

This wallpaper design inspired by a 17th-century chateau fresco is typically French, yet reminiscent of the arabesque-style decorative panels by Reveillon, which were popular a century later.

were reproduced on paper. Ornament was the next inspiration with every aspect of architectural detail from dado mouldings and friezes to columns and statues being made in paper.

Then came the innovation that people could make up the details themselves with décor – pilasters and panels with vertical and horizontal borders and figures or flowers as a centrepiece. This, together with the complete arabesque panels that were 1.8m (6ft) in height and designed to fit into panelling, were reserved for the grander homes. Typical designs featured scrolling leaves and flowers, ornament, figures and architectural landscapes. The popularity of scenic wallpapers depicting mythological scenes and paradise-like locations made up of several lengths to compose one panorama was short-lived.

The be-ribboned, be-garlanded designs, with twist and swags of fabric printed in the most delicate colours had a wider significance in ordinary homes, and basic styles live on to this day. Colours go in and out of fashion, new wipe-clean vinyls and innovations such as self-adhesive wallpapers may hit the high street but many of the designs are adaptations of these historic French designs.

NEO-CLASSICAL (LOUIS XVI 1765–1790)

As frequently happens when one fashion takes hold for a period of time, it is followed by a swing in a completely different direction. The transition from rococo was no exception, the move starting long before the accession of Louis XVI in 1774. Curved legs and scroll detail disappeared from chairs and cabinets to be replaced by straight, tapering shapes. A definite neo-classical style emerged. Furniture details were based on the architecture of ancient civilizations – Greek, Roman, Etruscan and Egyptian. Gone were the pretty floral and shell carvings; instead all motifs had a classical connection – urns, lions' masks, rams' heads, classical columns, Greek keys and honeysuckle.

Classical imagery like this continues to inspire designers today and crops up in all aspects of decor. Urns and columns are particular

Drape a Toile de Jouy fabric around a room and the effect is instantly French. But such extravagant displays are best reserved for the bedroom where drapery goes way back in history. Here three colourways work together harmoniously.

favourites of late, appearing in everything from stencilled walls to printed velvet fabrics.

Early printed French fabrics have become world classics. It was around this time that Toiles de Jouy fabrics started with classical imagery also featuring largely in these printed fabrics. In 1760, a fabric printing works was established in Jouy en Josas, near Versailles. The fabric used was cotton, purely because other cloths like silk, damask and brocade were subject to taxation whereas no tax was levied on printed cotton. The designs were typically pictorial with scenes inspired by mythology, Chinese or pastoral situations, many being undertaken by Huet. Nowadays we associate Toiles with a single colour on a neutral background but originally designs were printed in many colours.

DIRECTOIRE (1794–1804)

Directoire or Republicaine style came immediately after the French Revolution. Slight differences were beginning to take shape in furniture – pieces were smaller in scale and much simpler than the preceding Louis XVI era. Typical furnishings were asymmetrical curved-sided day beds while chairs had straight-edged seats

The French have a flair for classically simple interiors and this window treatment proves that curtains need not be elaborate to be effective. The tactile cream cotton draped over a pole adds instant elegance to this living room. The paisley top cloth on the corner table is likely to be a shawl – a look that was at its height of popularity in Napoleon's day.

and rectangular-shaped backs, which were the beginnings of Empire style.

EMPIRE FIRST (1801–1815)

France was rocked by the Revolution in 1789 and it was soon after, under the rule of Napoleon, that Empire style came into being. Brilliant, rich-coloured silks, luxurious drapes, fabric-covered rooms and gilt-decorated furniture were just a few hallmarks of this era. Furniture was generally unfussy and incorporated straighter lines with legs sometimes taking the form of a creature. Use was made of large expanses of decorative woods like cherry.

Again fashion played a part in chair design and the trend for ladies wearing narrow dresses led to narrower chair seats. Reclining was an acceptable relaxation position, hence the use of chaise longues or day-beds together with bolster cushions.

Curtains were decidedly dramatic. Fabric flowed and was draped over stunning poles. Trimmings were extravagant too – fringes and silky tassels completed the look. A double curtain arrangement became popular with an inner curtain of muslin and a heavier silk overcurtain. In the bedroom, canopies dressed the head of the bed.

There has been a recent revival of such ambitious window dressings although, in order to appeal to our age of DIY'ers who are well accustomed to labour-saving devices, mass manufacturers have introduced a crop of poles, drape hooks and curtain accessories to make successful drapery straightforward. 20th-century inventions such as touch-and-close tape make these tasks relatively simple.

The Empire style continued to be popular and style changes

were slow on the whole, although there was a tendency for mahogany to be replaced by lighter-coloured woods. Heavy buttoning and coil-sprung upholstery became the norm and several variations on a love-seat appeared.

19TH-CENTURY ROCOCO REVIVAL (LOUIS PHILLIPE XV 1830–1848; LOUIS XVI REVIVAL 1852–1870)

Interiors of the 19th century were very much a case of *déjà vu*, with favourite styles of the past being resurrected. Rococo was much in evidence again at the turn of the century. Empire-style chairs remained popular until the middle of the century and there was also a following of Louis XV and Louis XVI. As the bourgeoisie grew in the years following the Napoleonic wars, so did industrialization and the quality of French furniture between 1815 and 1850 dropped. Eventually France lost its position as fashion leader in decor.

ART NOUVEAU (C1890–1910)

This lack of progress continued as industrialization was slow and the country on the whole was still dependent on agriculture. Furniture was craft orientated and period styles still the norm. However, it was from France that signs of the first new style for decades was to emerge – art nouveau. With its curved lines and symbolism, shapes were sensuous and elegant. French artists Gallé and Lalique with their stunning glassware have been rated among the highest ranks of French masters of style. Hector Guimard also had a great influence on home design and his asymmetric flowing scrolls could be seen at all levels in the home from stained glass, fabric and wallpapers to furniture. His most famous input was on ironwork which was and is still used widely in France for gates, balconies and staircases.

It is perhaps Thonet's bentwood furniture that has made the greatest mark on French style as a whole over the years. Thonet, although Prussian born and initially working in Vienna, had considerable associations with France. His inspired furniture became a national institution and at one time the chairs became as

14 *French flavour can be added to any room; here a* Bonheur de jour *(lady's writing desk) transforms a redundant corner into a study. Hard floors like terracotta or wood help to set the scene.*

much a staple product in cafés and restaurants as baguettes and pastis. He was the first to perfect the mechanization of bending wood and it was because of the relatively low price of his furniture that it was adopted nationwide. It was not until many years later that bentwood became part and parcel of domestic interiors. Fashionable furnishing stores helped with the acceleration of this trend by making bentwood chairs available and appealing in innovative displays.

ART DECO (C1923–1935)

The style that followed in the mid 1920s and 1930s – art deco – took its name from the Paris Exhibition of 1925, Exposition de Art Decoratifs. Ideas were progressive and, in an effort to move away from furnishings of the past, decorated, carved and inlaid furniture was replaced by plainer surfaces and sleek lines. The overall tone was dramatic, even showy, using vivid colours and bold patterns, extravagant materials like lacquer, ebony, ivory, chrome and leather, with outrageous upholstery fabrics including jewel satins, furs and animal skins. Designers reacted against the earlier curvy forms and instead shapes were more geometric with Egyptian, Cuban and Aztec cultures among the design influences.

Some forward thinking artists of this time did turn to the past for inspiration. Two of the pioneers of the art deco movement, an architect Louis Sue, and painter, André Mare, worked together and produced a unique look. Sue *et* Mare's style was unusual in that it combined the geometric forms of cubism and bold colours of the time with familiar traits of the styles of Louis XV, Louis XVI and Louis Phillipe. The result was a selection of home products, from lamps and door furniture to armchairs and console tables, with flair and a flavour of the past, such as floral motifs and delightful inlays of precious materials like ebony and pearl.

Art deco glass is synonomous with the name René Lalique, who is renowned for his opalescent blue glass. However, his contribution on the home design front also included mirrors, lamps and textiles. Although he worked in the art nouveau style, he excelled in deco form.

Many of the best French textiles in the 1920s were designed by the painters Raoul Dufy and Sonia Delaunay. They were not immune from taking historical leads either and Raoul Dufy is well known for giving the original versions of Toiles de Jouy fabrics new life. Neither Dufy or Delaunay had much influence on French homes in general at the time although their work has had more impact since. Several of Delaunay's designs have been issued in later years, and one featuring large freehand diamonds and small squares was redrawn from her original sketches by the Liberty studio and became one of their classic designs.

It was Jean Lurçat who was the outstanding influence in tapestry design. Working for Aubusson from 1933, he made a deliberate decision to change the design direction, abolish realism and perspective, reduce the colour palette and make tones stronger. Instead he used motifs such as birds, fish, animals and trees as well as stars, suns and flames.

At the time, tubular steel furniture was in its infancy in Europe and the architect most closely linked with making it successful is Le Corbusier. Swiss by birth, architect by profession and designer by instinct, he was a man who had considerable French connections, and originally came to prominence in the 1925 Paris Exhibition which he furnished with Thonet bentwood chairs. Four years later, together with Charlotte Perriand, he produced his two most famous chairs – the chaise longue and the Grand Confort armchair, both of which were manufactured by Thonet.

Art deco and art nouveau have had more impact on interior design trends since their day. The intricate form of art nouveau meant that manufacturing en masse was complex and as such was short-lived, while the very nature of art deco with its luxurious materials made it out of reach of most of the population who continued to furnish their homes with period styles. It took the 1960s to bring art deco to the attention of the masses. If you now look in any contemporary French city apartment, the chances are that there will be some Le Corbusier inside.

1930S ONWARDS

The late 1930s and 1940s saw a wave of combined creative inspiration with ideas being exchanged between interior specialists, furniture manufacturers, fashion designers and artists. The style that defied the time of economic crisis with its clean lines, bold shapes and almost sculptural furnishings gives a dramatic glamour and is very much de rigueur in France at present. Designers revived and totally turned around some of the best elements of centuries before. Louis XVI influences like straight tapered legs, lute and lyre chairbacks, and rich velvets once again made an impact. But this style had a personality of its own – pale woods, creams and ivory colourways, fruitwood furniture, Venetian glass – combining clean lines and a light, elegant touch. The contradiction of the large box-

Chinoiserie was at its height in the early 18th century when entire rooms were given the Chinese treatment. In fresh blue and white, this wallcovering adds a flavour of the Orient without becoming overpowering. The washbasin, with its pretty fluted shape, is unmistakably French, from the time of Louis XV.

shaped furniture and delicate ironwork elements in tables, stools, sconces and lighting appeals to homemakers today. The work of designers Poillerat, Felix Davin, Andre Dubreuil and especially Jean Michel Frank, who is admired for his unexpected mix of luxurious and modest materials, crops up in the most stylish of French homes, frequently mixed with 18th or 19th century classics.

The most influential of French designers linked with the home in the last decade has to be Phillipe Starck, whose claim to fame was decorating a room in President Mitterand's home. Renowned for quirky yet practical versions of home basics, his most famous designs have been a kettle and a lemon squeezer.

So, although French style has seen many changes over the years, many elements have survived the centuries. The selection of interiors in this book shows just how the style may vary. But, by highlighting the details that are characteristic of individual rooms in each section, you should get a clue as to how to reconstruct a French flavour. Bear in mind that it is how the interiors are put together as much as what they contain that makes them distinctly French. It is certainly worth persevering with a project or two so that even if the Louis XV armchair is out of reach you can add that certain French flair by simple decor tricks like framing and arranging a group of pictures in the essential style *français*.

CHAPTER ONE

ESSENTIAL ELEMENTS OF STYLE

INSTALLING A SET OF LOUIS XVI ARMCHAIRS will not instantly translate a sitting room into French. Style encompasses expression as well as appearance, and even though introducing the right criteria helps, fulfilling the style properly involves far more.

When it comes to interiors, the way the space is used and what else goes into it are equally as important as the main French *'objets'*. Just as creating the right image with a particular fashion style relies on relevant basics and clever accessorizing, achieving the desired effect with home decor depends on a mix of essential ingredients and then adding the trimmings. Colour and texture are vital pieces in the style jigsaw.

Individual style choice is likely to be as much dictated by geographical area as by personal preferences. Regional differences in style are particularly marked in France. It is important when creating your own French look to adopt a style that suits the place you live in as well as your personality.

THE ESSENTIAL INGREDIENTS

Every country has an identity. If you cross a border into France or arrive in France without warning, you will not have to travel far before establishing your whereabouts. The clusters of shutter-clad houses, often bleak in appearance, are surrounded by land as opposed to fronted by cricket-pitch striped lawns, with no neat paths and quaint garden gates or picture windows to give a hint of what lies within. In this sense many French houses lack a magnetism that draws your curiosity and makes you long to step inside, but the spatter of scarlet geraniums punctuating the greyness of stone or granite walls, doorsteps, balconies and village memorials gives a clue that this is a nation of folk who care.

You seldom see an apology of a window box with vivid pink fuchsias fighting with fiery amber marigolds. The colours of the flowers you see work together. Here we have a nation of people who are aware of how things look, with some understanding of not

overdoing the effect so it becomes ugly.

The French care about their houses. But, more importantly, the house must be a home, a family centre. The dining table is to French homes what the coffee table is to a British home. It is part of the relaxation process, the place to congregate with friends to share a drink and exchange conversation.

Eating is a ritual all over France; TV dinners are discouraged. The whole of French home life centres around meals in the kitchen, although the arrangement is not necessarily formal. The scenario of the immaculately laundered tablecoth is not a daily occurrence, in fact mealtimes are more likely to be relaxed with a plastic-coated cloth thrown over the table and wine served in chunky tumblers – no crystal wine glasses, teapot, or bread basket, which are reserved for the dining room. Instead the baguette is conveniently served directly on the table, ready to be torn into hand-sized pieces by the diners to relish with a chunk of cheese or to dip into anything liquid from the salad dressing to the red wine.

Day-to-day living is a structured event with a regular two-hour break at midday, when folk never fail to slow down and stop

Nothing beats colour and texture for conjuring up a style and this hallway with its ceramic floor and weathered timbers breathes rural France. The palette of pastels with rose pink colourwashed wall, hyacinth blue woodwork and green garden bench adds welcome life to all the neutral tones.

20 *Even if there are no natural surfaces in your home, you can easily evoke a French country mood. A roughly plastered wall painted in lavender blue, simple furnishings and minimally dressed windows will suffice. Add piles of natural textures and 'age' the paint on furniture by sanding it down.*

everything to eat. Cramming in the shopping or paying the gas bill are rare lunchtime activities. Homes are similarly organized. Function is the keyword with furnishings being ultimately practical. Kitchens are kept in the manner found in hotels with a cooking implement and receptacle geared for every specific recipe and dish.

On the whole, furniture scale is large. Outsized armoires (wardrobes) are found in living areas as much as bedrooms, where they house crockery and table linen. Dainty coffee tables are rare; instead a solid sideboard or console table may sit against a wall providing storage for a lamp or glassware in addition to being a visual feature.

Bathrooms, too, are geared for serious grooming. *La toilette* is a vital start to the day and efficiently planned bathrooms are considered essential. A bidet is a more important consideration than a pretty wicker chair.

Casual chic perhaps best sums up the approach to home decor. Even the smartest of rooms has a warmth so that it never becomes an untouchable parlour with a 'dare-to-sit-on-me' sofa. The more polished rooms exude personality. From rich fruitwood furniture and warm wooden floors to rough plaster walls and mellow terracotta tiles, colour and texture play an all-important part in the distinctive characteristics of French furnishings.

COLOUR AND TEXTURE

We have come to associate specific uses of colour in decor with certain nationalities. Muted hues like slate blue have an immediate association with New Engand or Scandinavia. Hot spicy tones suggest Mexican or even Spanish interiors. But when we think of French use of colour, our thoughts turn to the country and to the south, Provence.

The quality of light is unique on the Mediterranean coast and colour and texture used within the home tend to stem from local sources. In a region where terracotta, stone floors and mellow pottery mingle with basket and ironwork, colours are complementary, from soft clay pinks and clay tones like coral and straw yellow to lavender blue and dappled grey. Teamed with this would be simple fabrics – unbleached calico, simple cotton prints, checks, stripes or Indiennes (Provençal prints). The look is unstructured. Unfinished walls are of natural stone or rough plaster in its natural state or, alternatively, washed with diluted paint to give a soft shimmer of colour. All these complement the rustic quality of the hand-crafted and skilfully carved furniture. Bright blue is commonly used for woodwork and furniture in the southern regions and in Brittany. Traditionally believed to ward off bad luck, it is also believed that the strong blue keeps flies away.

Directly opposite on the style scale lie the more sophisticated furnished houses, more common in urban areas. Here colours are likely to be stronger. Rich honey shades of ochre on walls provide a solid backdrop to fruitwood furniture; shades of red are favoured as is energetic-patterned wallpaper.

Opposite: Just a single piece of French furniture in a corridor or on a landing can make a style statement. A Provençal banquette (bench) with rush seat and frame painted in traditional olive green is perfect for a country look or for a more elegant effect.

The trend for colour preferences is fascinating and companies whose business revolves around colour know what sells best by location.

'The French,' said a director of a well-respected English fabric company, 'tend to buy colours cyclically. One year it will be blue and yellow for home furnishings, a few years later it's terracotta. And then, whatever the design, terracotta will sell. The British on the other hand are more predictable. They rarely change in taste and always show a preference for fabrics combining rose pink with soft grey-green.'

Like any fashion, the use of colour in decor changes over time. The trends stem from all sorts of influences, and are linked to some extent with the use of particular dyestuffs.

In France, it was Madame Pompadour who sparked off the tendency to use pastel colours in homes, especially pink in the bedroom. Bright green is the main colour associated with Empire fashion, used in conjunction with purples and yellows and usually set against a background of gold and white. Excavations at Pompeii were said to be the reason for the colours used in the neo-classical era – rich reds, yellows and lilacs – while the Russian ballet in 1909 introduced bright colours again – green, lilac, purple and orange. Orange, lilac and lime green were still in evidence 15 years later in art deco upholstery, used with cream and turquoise, all of which are now acknowledged as typical deco colours. White and black were a popular duo with one wall sometimes covered with a mirror. Choosing appropriate paint shades will help make a period look authentic although often a toned-down version of the original is easier to live with.

WALLS

Strong colours on walls combined with French fruitwood furniture especially in a hall or dining room will put the French stamp on any room; but where such dramatic effects would prove too dark, colourwash is a sensible alternative. By diluting the paint and applying it randomly so that brushmarks are left in the finish the result is a tonal effect which gives depth of colour without being too heavy (see page 71).

One of the most appealing things about the walls of French country farmhouses is their roughness, most being made from natural stone or rough plaster. Reproducing the effect of natural stone well is tricky although there are several specialist books explaining various techniques. Achieving the look of rough plaster is easier as well as being suited to more situations.

Patterned wallpaper reminiscent of the past is as popular as ever in France and there is a wide choice of designs to choose from inspired by several historic periods. For those who enjoy pattern but prefer not to have it from skirting to cornice, a stencil is another option, with many French classic styles available in high street stores.

FLOORS

There is no competition for solid floors in France and the French never cease to be amazed by other nations' apparent obsession with wall-to-wall carpeting, even in the bathroom. All sorts of natural flooring is now widely available and sourcing new or original slate, flagstones or woodblock to recreate a French ambience is not difficult. As for ceramic, the choice is endless. However, for locations where it is not practical or an alternative is sought from

choice, there is an army of lookalikes, some of which are so convincing that it is hard to tell a fake. Particularly effective are good-quality vinyls, either in tile or sheet form.

FURNITURE

Period furniture remains popular in France. Many traditional styles are reproduced faithfully in cherrywood, with beds and dining room furniture boasting the greatest variety of styles. Recently, however, painted furniture has had an increased following and, while original pieces are extremely hard to trace, several manufacturers offer French-inspired country furniture, particularly for the kitchen or dining room, in the shape of dressers, shelves, draining racks, and bread cupboards. The paintwork is usually distressed to give the impression of age.

The ultimate item of French furniture has to be the armoire. This enormous wardrobe was often presented as part of the wedding dowry and passed down from one generation to the next.

FABRICS

Fabric does not tend to feature as voluminously in French homes as in British. Windows opening inwards make elaborate curtains impractical and unnecessary. Instead, lace set close to the glass or elegant drapes on poles, the simpler the better, are favoured. All through the home the French tend to favour natural fibres; cotton and linen reign for bedding, while polyester is suffered by some for its convenience but usually in moderation.

Upholstery fabrics keep apace with the times. Where once brocades and velvets would have been used, today a cotton weave is an acceptable alternative. Tapestries have long been associated with France and are still used to an extent on furniture and curtains but more so on wallhangings and cushions. Many of the styles sold in the high street today have their origins in 17th-century classic woven textiles. Contemporary fabrics at the window are frequently cream or sometimes striped, while Provençal prints in hot colours still earn their place, particularly in the kitchen, and Provençal quilts originally used as bedding are just as likely to be seen thrown over a sofa where they can be appreciated by all.

In order to give a room a French identity using fabric alone, the choice has to be a Toile de Jouy fabric. The distinctive etched designs, popular in the late 18th and 19th centuries, typically featured pastoral and mythological scenes in one colour on a neutral background and have become classics reproduced by many of the major fabric companies.

WINDOWS

There are two extremes of window treatments prevalent in France. At one end of the scale are the rural cottage windows which have a simple lace curtain and painted woodwork. At the other end of the scale are the elaborate window drapes of Empire style, complete with trimmings and tassels.

To emulate French style at its most elaborate, you should carry the period style throughout the room together with Empire colours – vivid greens, reds and golds. The whole look does, however, require a large, light room. Alternatively, you could compromise by using the exquisite French trimmings more selectively.

Less structured window treatments are more sympathetic to the majority of homes. Try dressing your windows in a mix of

Opposite: Mosaic pots like these, known as pique assiettes *(literally translated as 'plate stealing'), are highly collectable in France. Grouped together the composition works especially well, firstly because of the combination of shapes and sizes and secondly as a kaleidoscope of colour against the neutral stone wall and rich timber of the 18th-century chest. Below: Cotton lace panels are a regular companion to the characteristic shuttered windows of France. Stretched taut across the glass they let in maximum light and allow the intricate design to be fully appreciated.*

Charming blue and white checked curtains bring the freshness of the Midi into any home. Hung from a basic curtain rail, the look is kept clean and uncluttered. The cherrywood classic dining chairs add a final French touch.

distinctive Provençal cottons. With the vast selection of prints based on similar dyes the potential for mixing and matching is endless and lots of different designs work together successfully.

Those who prefer less pattern will prefer a simple timeless window dressing and for one that brings a breath of France into the home you cannot beat billowing blue and white checked curtains: sill-skimming for cottage charm, floor length for a more sophisticated touch. Or, for the ultimate French window, set up some shutters outside and stretch a crunchy cotton lace panel across the window panes inside.

DISPLAY

Many French people have an inherent natural flair for choosing and displaying pieces in the home, and a knack, not only of mixing old and new, but of arranging objects with care to make up a composition of shape and form that is pleasing to the eye.

The secret of successful accessorizing lies primarily in the way that objects work together. Even in a collection of things that are totally unrelated, careful mixing of scales and a blending of textures can all help. Finished arrangements should seldom seemed contrived, but instead should look harmonious.

Useful objects may double as a display feature by accident – the battery of copper pans hanging from a kitchen beam are not chosen by the French for their aesthetics but because copper is rated way above non-stick for cookware by this nation of ardent cooks. The pans just happen to be hanging to hand ready for daily use and the fact that they look wonderful in the process is a lucky aside. The set of enamelled containers on the kitchen shelf may be battered and far from new, but the weathered appearance in a French country kitchen is a positive visual attribute. The more used items are, the better – right down to the blackened kitchen stove.

Anything precisely positioned in a room, to the extent of being posed, automatically looks unapproachable; it is this lived-in appeal so common in French homes that makes us feel comfortable with what greets the eye. It is important, though, that the surroundings are sympathetic. A haphazard arrangement of dented cookware does not look quite the same in a pristine fitted glass-fronted cupboard as hanging against a rough stone wall.

Walls are the obvious focus of visual attention. Pictures need to be appreciated at eye level which means that in living rooms, where most time is spent sitting in low chairs, pictures should be positioned lower than in a corridor or hallway. One large picture or several smaller ones can set the mood, but they shoud be grouped together rather than scattered around the room or floating in space.

Pictures are not the only things that work on wall displays – fabric hangings, rugs, ceramics or sculptures all work in this way. Outline is the crucial ingredient.

The more you look the more you see in this room belonging to French interior designer Jacques Grange, who has a knack of combining relics of various eras to great effect.

THE FINAL LOOK

Arriving at a French style outside the French borders is not always easy. But creating a French-inspired style is. It may be impossible to track down or afford that Empire bed of your dreams but you can arrive somewhere near it by pushing a basic divan against a wall, setting up a draped effect and painting the walls in vivid green. Similar short cuts will give the flavour of a French kitchen, living room, bedroom, bathroom, or hall – even if the ambience is lacking. The result is more original and more satisfying if the style is not too structured.

Chapter Two

Halls and Entrances

There are a few things frowned upon by the French – one is rushing a meal, and another is crossing the threshold wearing a pair of high heels. Stilettos and wooden floors are just not compatible, and there are acres of timber-floored halls in France that risk being ruined if house rules are not followed. Visitors are often encouraged to slip off any footwear at the doorstep, transfer to sole-shaped fabric pads and glide about the house, conveniently polishing the surface of the floor as they do so. Where it is not wood, the hall floor will often be ceramic; there are some magnificent examples of traditional tiles and styles around to be looked after and treasured so that generations ahead can appreciate the craftsmanship and materials of the past.

SOLID FLOORING

Solid floors are the norm in hallways. They turn an ordinary hall into an impressive entrance which is easy to maintain; in addition a tiled floor looks appealing and can create an illusion of space. The

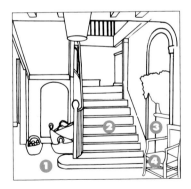

1 *Chequered ceramic floor*
2 *Exposed staircase*
3 *Console table*

4 *Rush-seated French country chair*

Timber used en masse never fails to create a favourable atmosphere and there is certainly plenty in this hallway with floorboards, sideboard, door and occasional chair all in polished wood. The wrought iron grille on the glass panelled door is typically French.

secret is to have tiles or blocks laid on the diagonal, thus taking the eye to each far corner of the hall, thereby seeming to widen the area. A combination of black and white chequered tiles are particularly popular in most geographical regions except in Provence where local tiles made from terracotta-coloured clay of the area are more commonly used.

Floorboards are sometimes left in their natural state, with just wax or varnish added for protection. Parquet flooring is also popular. These geometrically laid hardwood blocks never fail to look good. More recent versions of parquet are less painstaking to fit being pre-fixed to plywood, a system designed to make laying speedy and straightforward. Some of the more beautiful examples of parquet are comprised of blocks made from several different types of wood so that the overall colour and timber grain is varied.

It is more usual to see hall floors completely exposed, although recent years have seen an increased interest in using oriental carpets as runners in hallways. There is a vast choice of styles and colours from the less expensive flat-weave cotton kelims to hand-made rugs produced by traditional methods mainly from the weaving regions of Persia, Turkey, Afghanistan and parts of North Africa.

WALLS

Hall walls should be left with minimum cover. Many French hall walls are stone, which in its raw state is texturally pleasing. In some rooms a stone or bare plaster wall may be battened and lined with fabric but in the hallway, which is a thoroughfare, this is not

This farmhouse hallway in the Tarn et Garonne region of south-west France proves that rough walls and floors need not be cold and uninviting. Instead the mellow colouring and open texture of the local stone, complemented by the bleached timber beam and weathered column in the adjoining vestibule, make an entrance that positively glows with character and warmth. The intricate ironwork shelf support looks even more appealing for its layers of tawny rust and the swirling form echoes the filigree chandelier and charming door handle. The pair of wheat sheaves adds a symbolic touch, wishing prosperity on all who enter the home.

considered a priority. Where paint is used on plastered walls, use natural tones of colour from cream and buff to richer buttermilk.

OCCASIONAL FURNITURE

The hall is one of the few areas of a French home where you might find pieces of furniture used for display rather than function. This could take the form of a simple rustic hall table or a more ornate console table, perhaps with a marble top, elaborate legs and carved detail, but in either case providing nothing more than a surface for the morning mail, a jug of flowers and a hat, and a drawer to keep the keys.

A Provençal bench or banquette is an attractive piece of furniture originating from the southern region of Provence. The most characteristic of these banquettes have rush seats and, although they were once located by the fireside, are often now installed in the hallway where they look good but tend to become a dumping ground for coats and bags rather than a useful seating area. The more delicate wrought iron garden seats are further variations on benches found in hallways. These look particularly effective when used in conjunction with a tiled floor. Large sculptures – even statues – can make a stunning feature in such large open hallways with ceramic flooring.

If possible, the emphasis should be on furniture that is more useful than a bench. Where space allows, a good choice would be an armoire or a commode (chest of drawers) to hold the family possessions. The armoire is traditionally made from fruitwood or walnut, and was usually intricately carved with symbolic motifs like corn, hearts, doves and bunches of grapes or, alternatively, hand-painted with simplistic motifs like flowers, fruit and ribbons. The traditional Provençal armoire would have a top referred to as '*Chapeau de Gendarme*', so called because the arched central piece resembles the shape of a policeman's helmet. Painted furniture was owned by those who could not afford carved pieces. Inevitably the paint faded and wore over time but this distressed look has come to be loved as part of the character of the piece so much so that this

Opposite: In a spacious hallway there is usually somewhere to squeeze in a 'useful' piece of furniture. This three-drawer chest looks particularly handsome and is a clever contemporary interpretation of a traditional theme – a classical Louis XVI style brought into the 20th century with a dash of emerald green wood stain. Painted stair risers and a claret-coloured oriental rug introduce further colour and make a completely original decor.

Opposite: The iron balustrade and distinctive stone floor go a long way to ensuring that this hallway is a stunning interior feature, but the input of eminent French interior designer Jacques Grange, adding voluminous silk curtains, a dramatic curved-ended sofa and smart day bed, all in pure cream, ensure that the elegance is carried throughout the whole area.

look has become fashionable and new pieces of furniture are now made to look old. Commodes or chests come in all shapes, sizes and finishes from bow-fronted decorative pieces to plain rustic styles.

Where a hall is furnished and has one or more windows it can become more akin to a living room than a corridor. However, hall windows should never be overdressed. Half-glazed front doors are frequent, the glass usually screened with a lace panel or ironwork.

The French hall does not tend to serve as a general family storage area. So make sure wellington boots are stashed away, and coats are hung out of sight.

Where there is a free wall there is a place for a mirror. The hall is ideal for siting one in a convenient position for last-minute adjustments to personal appearance before venturing outside.

LIGHTING

For first impressions, nothing beats appropriate lighting and, as no specific activity happens in the hallway, there is little need for strong illumination. Softer mood lighting is effective, wall-mounted candle fittings being a popular choice.

IRONWORK

Curvaceous ironwork appears in various guises in a French home, from wine carriers to shelf brackets, window boxes to balconies, but is perhaps at its most impressive in hallways where it is often used simply as a means of decorating the glass of windows and doors. Also used for more elaborate applications, iron can be used to make decorative staircases and magnificent candelabras.

STAIRS

Bare floorboards are the norm in French homes. Being accustomed to hard floors throughout the house, the French find little need to cover the staircase. They are well-used to the only disadvantage that goes hand in hand with traffic up and down exposed treads – constant noise – and consider it worth tolerating when the option would mean covering up a handsome architectural feature.

$\mathcal{P}$ROJECTS

SCENTED DOOR BOUQUET

Herbs are not confined to the kitchen in France – apart from having a bunch to hand to flavour the béchamel sauce – they are enjoyed for their aroma elsewhere. Make up a herbal bouquet and hang it on the front door on a day when you are expecting visitors.

You will need

❋

- Selection of garden herbs of various colours and textures
- Elastic band
- Scissors
- Raffia or sisal string

4 *Tie some raffia or sisal string around the stems and hang the bouquet upside down on the front door.*

2 *Lay the large-leaved plants on a flat surface. Then arrange plants in layers on top, using the spikier varieties to give structure and the softer edged plants like geranium and forget-me-not to fill the gaps.*

1 *Collect together a group of fresh herbs. Try to include plants with varied leaf sizes and type, flowering and non-flowering, keeping stems of each as long as possible. For a pleasing composition use some large-leaved herbs like sage, spiky-leaved plants like rosemary and lavender, and some with irresistible perfumes like lemon balm and scented geranium, as well as a small frothy plant like forget-me-not – this will be useful as a 'filler'.*

3 *When you have a pleasing arrangement, secure the stems together with an elastic band and trim the ends of the stems to the same length.*

RUSTIC PAINTED CUPBOARD

Step into a traditional French household and the chances are that before you get very far you will come across a characterful armoire in polished wood or well worn paint. You can immediately capture the feeling of a French home with a large cupboard like this and a spacious hallway is the perfect location. But to recreate the character can be tricky. If you cannot find a timber original, you can transform any cupboard, old or new, into a piece of furniture with a personality of its own.

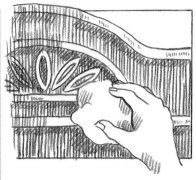

You will need

- Decorator's brushes
- Old cupboard or wardrobe
- Eggshell paint
- Pre-tinted glaze (available from specialist paint and DIY stores)
- Dragging brush
- Rag
- Jigsaw
- Staple gun

2 *Take a dragging brush – a long-bristled brush – and pull it through the wet glaze to create soft straight lines.*

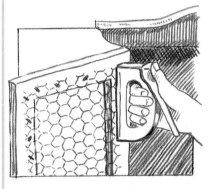

3 *Leave to dry for 15 minutes then, taking a rag, gently wipe off the glaze on corners and mouldings. Leave to dry.*

1 *Paint an old cupboard or wardrobe with a coat of a light-coloured eggshell paint and leave to dry. Then apply tinted glaze evenly over the surface, brushing in one direction only.*

4 *To create a Provençal style on a panelled cupboard, remove the central panel using a jigsaw and replace it with chicken wire, fixing it to the inside with a staple gun.*

CHAPTER THREE

DINING ROOMS

IF A GLANCE AT ESTATE AGENTS' LITERATURE gives a hint as to how people use their houses, you would be forgiven in thinking that dining rooms are a dying breed. Billed instead as family room, playroom, utility room, TV room or cloakroom for much of the time, a room devoted solely to eating comes way down the list of priorities in many countries. Not so in France. Dining rooms live on in a big way. They may be informal with a cotton cloth covering up a well-worn table, or extra smart with a handsome polished table and matching chairs. Whatever the arrangement, the chances are that the dining room will be very much in evidence.

When planning a French-style dining room, there is one rule of thumb: the room must not be so formal that it becomes foreboding. Dining the French way is an afternoon or evening's entertainment and as such should be enjoyed in comfort.

1 *Classic cane-backed dining chairs*
2 *Vaisselier (dresser) laden with useful china*
3 *Ceramic floor*
4 *Rich fruitwood side table*

provides a surface for serving and an area for display
5 *White linen tablecloth makes dining more of an occasion*
6 *Collection of glassware ready for the selection of wines*

40 *Dining is very often an informal affair but always an occasion. This dining area in a corner of a Breton cottage looks particularly welcoming with its carved banquette (bench) against the rough stone wall and the table laid with a cheerful checked and fringed cloth plus Provençal print napkins. Note the lovely encaustic tiles on the floor near the door.*

FURNITURE

Anyone wanting to create an especially chic dining room could not do better than follow a classic French style. A wide choice of reproduction furniture exists. For a more formal look, chairs modelled on 18th-century styles – Louis XV and XV1 – featuring decoratively carved arms and legs with elegant upholstery and polished, gilt or painted frames set the scene. Timbers would originally have been walnut, maple, cherry or sometimes beech which was painted or varnished. Chairs with upholstered backs come in a variety of shapes – square, rectangular or shield – echoing styles of the mid-18th century

For a more informal setting, dining chairs emulating French provincial styles are the best choice. Primarily made from fruitwood like walnut, often combined with cane or rush seats, the texture softens the appearance. Those with plain slatted backs are associated with the earlier period and those with detailed backs in the shape of lyres, wheatsheaves and wooden basketwork the later years of Louis XVI.

For a more rustic French look, choose curvaceous iron or basic country kitchen timber chairs, even benches. They can be brightened up with a coat of paint or with pretty cushions.

FABRICS

Colourful cotton fabrics are perfect. Ideal for cheering up a country dining room, they are the easiest way of adding a flavour of France in any home as they are so readily available. The characteristic Provençal prints with their small motifs in hot spice shades were copied from 17th-century Indian hand-blocked prints – Indiennes – which were first manufactured over two centuries ago in Tarascon. Styles have changed slightly over the years. Under the reign of Louis XVI and after the Revolution, flowers, vines and herbs printed on a terracotta background were the order of the day. During the *Directoire* period, prints were more stylized with geometric designs in plums and olive green, while in the early 19th century patterns took the shape of tiny motifs like circles.

Provençal-style fabrics are equally adored today and most retailers offer some version of the French country story in home furnishings, especially tableware. More recently, cotton checks and striped fabrics, especially in cobalt blue and white, have been associated with this look.

The main difference between French and English country style is probably the use of frills. On the whole, French soft furnishings are more tailored; to reproduce a French country dining area accurately with fabric, simplicity is the key. Mix and match prints for maximum impact but keep shapes square and edges straight – no valances or scallops and definitely no frills.

A splash of yellow and blue paint together with some typical Provençal country fabrics and metal chairs leave us in no doubt that this dining room is modelled on French style.

WALLS

Paintwork to complement this look should go in one of two directions – either dramatic-coloured woodwork or roughly-textured white walls. Alternatively, tongue-and-groove panelling fits the bill well, evoking a certain coastal feel, but is best painted a strong colour.

In grander houses, original wood panelling makes an elegant setting in which to eat, while fabric lining the walls, a technique that has been popular for centuries, remains a firm favourite as an alternative wallcovering to paper. The easiest way to achieve this look without going to the great lengths and cost involved in fixing fabric to wooden battens, is to carry through the same design and colourway all around walls and windows, on paper and fabric. Early wallcoverings were made for this very reason, to mimic the drapery which they did so exactly and resulted in some very clever *trompe l'oeil* effects. Today a repetition of the same printed pattern is sufficient without the visual trickery of folds, pleats and drapes.

In the first half of the 18th century, dining room walls were often covered with red velvet or paper imitating the fabric. Flock was popular for borders, giving the effect of textile braid. Later in the century architectural features were created in paper, and columns, dado friezes and ornaments like cherubs were pasted to the wall. All these elements are available in stencils today and they lend themselves admirably to a classic dining room. Some clever three-dimensional impressions can be achieved with stencils by building up layers in progressive tones. It is relatively straightforward to create a mock panelled effect with architectural stencils although it is important to mark the wall first to ensure that the corners are square. Paint the area inside the border a slightly deeper tone than the surround to enhance the idea of relief.

FLOORS

Wooden flooring is and has always been common in French dining rooms, either woodblock or plain floorboards. If you are considering the laborious task of stripping floorboards to achieve this style, it is

worth checking out the vinyl lookalikes which are extremely convincing. They also involve much less effort and mess into the bargain.

GLASSWARE

A French-style dining room should include at least one other piece of furniture to house china, glassware and linen. The French have always been fond of their glassware although the glass-making industry as such was recognized to be behind the rest of Europe in skill and originality. Design was of Venetian influence with factories being run by Italian immigrants. In the mid-18th century, the now famous Baccarat factory was founded which started off the trend for rich-coloured vessels. Silver has been a national passion for centuries too, and some of the most typical French silverware was made in the 18th century and includes delightful implements like wine tasters – small bowls with an S-shaped handle.

Wooden floors are favoured by the French but, where the genuine article is not possible, a lookalike vinyl is a superb alternative. This stripwood flooring has been laid on the diagonal and highlighted with silver inserts to make the area seem wider. The chairs designed by Jean Charles de Castelbajac for Ligne Roset with the bizarre name of My Funny Valentine, are inspired by an 18th-century salon furnished with Louis XVI chairs with oval medallion-shaped backs covered in floral tapestries.

LINEN

Table linen, too, has had pride of place since the 17th century although now a French family will happily substitute a freshly laundered cloth for fabric place mats. Traditionally linen was used daily, the white damask cloth being the stalwart of all times and has been in use since the 17th century. At this time it was figured with exquisite patterns made up of pictorial images like historical, religious or hunting scenes, together with flowers and fruit. The partial satin sheen of damask contrasting with matt areas gives it a luxurious touch and light reflection that has appealed to generations of diners. Today damask is used as a collective term for all sturdy traditional table linen and is frequently woven in several tones of a few colourways and in an easy-care yarn.

In French country homes, glass-fronted cupboards or vast dressers, often elaborately carved, housed the china and glassware. Without fail, a piece like this today will be similarly laden with ceramics that are used on a regular basis. Dressers are rarely reserved for display only.

Sometimes a more compact sideboard or buffet would replace a dresser; there are many rural pieces dating from the 18th century. Early examples were chunky and plain with no bulky knobs or fussy detail, cupboard doors being opened with a key only. Knobs were small on drawers. Apart from lacy brass ferrules that sometimes followed the length of the door, nothing else interrupted this neat shape.

Reproduction dining room furniture follows more elegant styles, again mainly in fruitwood. This has the advantage of a rich colour and interesting grain yet is not as cumbersome as some of the more rustic pieces or as overbearing as mahogany or oak, so is especially suited to more restricted spaces. Good manufacturers concentrate on authenticity as well as quality, including period detail so that a buffet representing the Directoire period would have visible dowelling, lozenges and ebony marquetry border, plus brass shoes for feet.

So, in the French dining room it is a case of history repeating itself. It is interesting that contemporary furniture designers still turn to the past for inspiration. One witty interpretation by Jean Charles de Castelbajac for Ligne Roset in a combination of strong-coloured fabrics was inspired by Louis XVI chairs in an 18th-century salon. France of the past will no doubt continue to influence designers of the future. In the dining room, the linen will continue to be stored en masse, pottery piled up and glassware galore stacked at the ready. All in preparation for a *grand repas*.

Opposite: With its china blue painted tongue-and-groove panelling teamed with white paint and crisp blue and white gingham, this dining room has a distinct coastal flavour typical of Brittany. The pair of glass-fronted door screened with curtains contribute to the clean-edged decor and, at the same time, are a canny way of concealing a pile of dining room paraphernalia like crockery, glassware and linen.

$\mathcal{P}$ROJECTS

MOCK WALLPAPER

The least expensive way of creating a wallpaper look is to use a stencil, spacing motifs far apart. Choose a simple design in one colour; the fleur-de-lis emblem is ideal as a representation of France, being the royal coat of arms since the 12th century and applied to the kings' furniture over the centuries. The feudal overtones led to it being banned during the Revolution. The fleur-de-lis itself is derived from a lily shape and its graphic outline looks particularly stunning in gold on a dark-coloured wall like red, or red on buff. Red was traditionally used for dining room walls. You can buy a commercial stencil from a specialist stencil store or, if you prefer, cut your own design from scratch.

You will need
❋

- Pencil
- Fleur-de-lis stencil
- Spray adhesive
- Deep red or gold stencil paints or artist's acrylics
- Saucer
- Stencil brush
- Paper towel

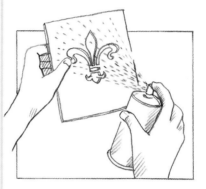

2 *Spray the reverse of the stencil with spray adhesive and place it on the wall in one of the marked positions.*

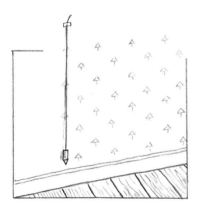

1 *Using a pencil, mark out the positions for the fleur-de-lis motifs on your wall. Make sure they are equally spaced and staggered for an all-over pattern.*

3 *Pour a little paint in a saucer and dip the stencil brush into it. Dab the brush on a paper towel to remove excess paint.*

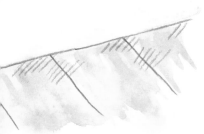

4 *Work the brush in a circular motion through the stencil to apply the paint. Then remove the stencil, reposition it and apply more paint.*

PAINTED SIDE TABLE

A side table makes a convenient resting place in a dining room for ceramics, glassware and wine. Delicate flowers on an olive green background were commonly seen on Provençal furniture of the 18th century. Follow the steps of this project to recreate this look today.

You will need

- Decorator's brush
- Old table
- Cream or dark green eggshell paint
- Motifs from books, wrapping paper or wallpaper
- Carbon paper

- Soft pencil
- Chalk (optional)
- Artist's oil paints
- Artist's paintbrush
- Gold stencil stick

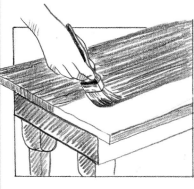

1 *Paint the table with a coat of eggshell paint and leave to dry thoroughly.*

2 *Look through sources — books, magazines or wrapping paper — for a suitable motif that could be reproduced in paint and is the correct proportion for the table. You can enlarge or reduce it in size using a photocopying machine but it has to be the right shape. Choose a simple picture with a strong outline and minimal detail.*

continued over ➤

48

3 *Trace the outline of the design onto carbon paper using a soft pencil. Lay the carbon paper on the table and transfer the image onto the table by redrawing over the pencil lines on the carbon paper. If you have painted the table with a dark colour, you will need to rub chalk on the back of the carbon paper so that the design shows up.*

4 *Using artist's oil paints and an artist's paintbrush, carefully fill in the detail of the chosen motifs.*

5 *When the decoration is thoroughly dry, add the antiquing effect. Rub the gold stencil stick over the moulding using your thumb or forefinger. The slight sheen makes the surface look shabby. (This works especially well on mouldings or turned legs and is a good way of breaking up solid colour and adding highlights.)*

GROUPING PICTURES

An easy way to conjure up a French style in a formal dining room is to make a feature of several pictures on the wall. Start by making sure that the set of pictures makes a harmonious group. They need not all be of the same style but it helps if the frames are similar, and should preferably include an element of gilt. Give a contemporary picture frame a period look with DIY gilding. It is often cheaper to buy a cheap print and re-use the frame rather than buy a purpose-made frame. All the materials listed below are available from specialist decorators' suppliers.

You will need
❁

- Picture frames
- Primer (if picture frames are untreated)
- Gold size
- Soft artist's paintbrush
- Gold metallic powder
- Soft dusting brush or make-up brush
- Protective mask

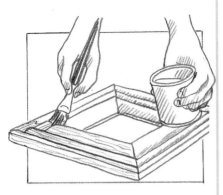

1 If the frames are untreated, prime first with commercial primer. Brush gold size thinly onto the frames using a large soft artist's brush.

2 When the size is tacky but nearly dry, brush on gold powder using a soft dusting brush. It is advisable to wear a protective mask when doing this as the fine powder can get everywhere. When the frames are dry, brush off the loose gold dust.

3 Now group the pictures carefully. Hang the pictures fairly close to each other as large gaps will break the grouping effect. Judge the amount of space that is best for each individual picture. The livelier the picture in content and colour, the more space it will need around it.

4 Do not be tempted to hang too high – remember that the pictures will be viewed at eye level, which in a dining room will be when you are seated at the table. Lastly, accessorize with panache. Choose dining room accessories that complement the picture group – a gilt candelabra, a gilt-based side lamp, simple table linen that does not fight with the pictures, and gold-rimmed plates.

CHAPTER FOUR

*L*IVING ROOMS

51

YOU COULD SAY THAT A FRENCH LIVING ROOM is the exact opposite of an English one. A smart Normandy salon will be as streamlined as its channel neighbour's living room is frilly; it will lack rose-strewn chintzes, deep pile carpet, frills and valances and instead boast tailored furniture, silks or brocades, and classic rugs. Streamlined, yet never stark, the French living room is organized for relaxation, with furniture positioned and grouped in such a way that

1 *18th-century French neo-classical sofa*
2 *Shuttered French windows have been painted and distressed for an antiqued look*
3 *Simple silk swags are the only window dressing*
4 *Classic Louis XV armchairs with carved frames feature stylized shells*
5 *Louis XIV-style table with lion-carved legs*
6 *Empire-style lamp with swan motifs supporting candle fittings*

7 *Turkish carpet*
8 *Grand candelabra*
9 *Mixture of textures – silks, velvets, brocades, toiles and embroidered fabrics – mingle well together*
10 *Trio of pictures make a feature by linking together with rope*
11 *Walls painted in burnt orange have been distressed to soften and give the impression of age*
12 *An impressive gesso statue makes the ultimate accessory*

A grand sitting room with Empire overtones, typified by the classic inspiration, folding Roman currule-style stools, plus the representations of animals in the furniture legs from lions' masks to the pawed feet of tables. The symmetrical arrangements of candlesticks and pairs of lions is also characteristic of this style, which is still a favourite in modern-day France.

serious reading is as feasible as an afternoon snooze, and conversation as practical as watching television.

FURNITURE

The multi-function facility of the French living room sometimes stretches to eating, with the room doubling as a dining room and becoming one general living area, although in instances where it does exist in its own right, it is very much this civilized arrangement that is prevalent. It is in the living room that you will come across the widest variety of furnishing types often stemming from a range of different eras. There tends to be a high proportion of armchairs compared with sofas but, however diverse the styles and shapes, the entirety will seldom look bitty.

Traditional-style furniture has remained a firm favourite with the French over the decades but a young couple setting up home today would be as likely to mix a pair of antique-style chairs with a contemporary sofa for their basic furnishings. Styles based on Le Corbusier and Thonet classic bentwood chairs have a timeless appeal and crop up over and over again in homes all over France, while 1940s style is considered very much *de rigueur* and the designer Jean-Michel Frank is a major design influence.

FABRICS

Upholstery is commonly a mingle of textures too. You could have a tapestry-covered chair jostling with a brocade and a modern cotton weave all in one living room. Needlepoint was frequently worked as upholstery in the early 18th century, mostly in florals although Point'Hongrie, a striking geometric design, was a well-used stitch of the time. The most straightforward way of arriving at a similar

needlepoint look in a living room today is to work a pattern in a traditional design using yarn on canvas, and make it up into cushions or use it as a chairback – the perfect ruse for adding period flavour to more contemporary furnishings. Throws are a clever way of bridging the era gap; mid-19th century quilts made from striking Provençal cotton prints will add a flash of French character to a contemporary sofa. Interestingly, the trend in France most recently has been the opposite – to accessorize the old with new and offset classic French furniture with avant-garde art and sculptures.

Armoires and French homes go hand in hand. These capacious cupboards are as commonplace today in the living room or dining room as in the bedroom, and they are used to store household essentials from linen to china and glass.

The visual impact of this living room with adjoining dining area is very much due to the interplay of textures: the raw silk curtains with crunchy tassels, the weighty Indian-inspired cotton quilt covering the table, kelim- and velvet-covered armchairs, and the glistening bone china, pewter and gold lustre cups in the cupboard on the far wall. The olive green paintwork on the cupboard interior picks up the colour of the painted vases standing on top as well as complementing the ochre hues in the upholstery, and makes the perfect backdrop for the contents. Used against the elegant Wedgwood blue of the panels, it is a somewhat unexpected colour combination but one that works successfully.

Damask, the main drawing room upholstery fabric of the 18th century, remains a firm favourite and, being readily obtainable, is an obvious route to French style at its most classic. Used either as curtains or upholstery, en masse it can become visually overpowering; but trimmings and textured cushions will relieve the density.

Brocade will suffice in that it gives a similar look, the difference being that damask is reversible with the design on both sides. Tapestry, a 19th-century favourite, is sold off the roll as a ready-made upholstery fabric for covering cushions or stools. Just adding touches of these will accentuate the French element in a living room.

FIREPLACES

Fireplaces have always been important as a focal point of a room and today they are valued as much for their display facility as heat emission. A cottage in the provinces might have a stone fireplace or even a vast inglenook which would originally have provided cooking facilities. The sophisticated living room, on the other hand, would be likely to feature a marble variety, possibly of Empire style, complete with lion's feet at the base of the pillars. Over the mantel, without fail, would be a grand mirror.

Marble-look fireplaces today made from resin provide cheaper alternatives while it is not difficult to achieve a grand look with the simplest timber or MDF (medium density fibreboard) fireplace kit. All it takes is the right materials, a feather and a comprehensive and inspirational book on paint finishes and you can recreate a marble effect with paint.

MIRRORS

It is thanks to the French, for their invention of glass casting in the late 17th century, that large mirrors exist. By pouring molten glass into a metal plate and rolling it flat quickly, it was possible to produce mirrors of even thickness and a large size that had previously been impossible. Since then, a sizeable mirror has been a standard fitting in French sitting rooms and inevitably plays a central role in the room design. Mirror frames reflect interior styles as much as furniture and French mirrors are easily identifiable. Those from the rococo period feature enthusiastic scrolls, curves, flowers, even candlesticks, whereas an Empire style would include inlays, veneers, swags, beading and classical urns.

WINDOW DRESSINGS

Many houses and apartments in France are blessed with high ceilings and impressive windows. Although we associate the French with lavishly draped curtains, today the emphasis tends to be on fabric quality rather than on elaborate dressing; window treatments are usually kept minimal, arranged at their most dramatic in basic swags to complement without dominating the shuttered windows. Decorative impact as such will be achieved with details like exquisite fringed edging or chunky tasselled tie-backs using some of the finest examples of trimmings. Fabrics nowadays are commonly understated, with plain cottons, silks or sheers being greatly favoured. Cotton prints are found in the French country home where checks or Provençal designs are part of the interior scene.

Toiles de Jouy, the classic French furnishing fabric printed in one colour on neutral cotton background, does not feature largely in

Toile de Jouy, the queen of French fabrics with its delightful pictorial representations, can be appreciated fully in this living room stretched on a screen and made into cushions where the design is much more clearly visible than on fully gathered curtains. The cushions are made from three antique toiles, the screen from a modern interpretation by Percheron. Identical-sized pictures look brilliant in quantity; the subject matter is almost irrelevant – it is the grouping that creates the feature.

living room furnishings; its use is more generally confined to bedroom drapes. Original toiles, however, are much treasured, being valued for their antique worth, and are more likely to be used as a wallhanging, a sofa throw or cushion covers where their beauty can be appreciated, rather than hanging at the window.

WALLS

Fabric-lined walls have long been a trademark of the French. This practice was at its prime in Napoleon's day when entire rooms, including windows and ceilings, were decked with fabric creating a complete tented effect. Even now it is not unusual for the most modest of homes to use fabric fixed to the walls, albeit of different quality from the exquisite textiles used by grander French homes.

Today you could opt for a compromise between the convenience of hanging a wallpaper and the appeal of texture akin to a fabric by choosing a velour wallcovering.

FLOORS

The floor of the living room could be ceramic or wood, and scattered with rugs. Alternatively, you could choose a classic traditional French carpet, styled after those made in Aubusson and Savonnerie in the 17th and 18th century. The designs most associated with Aubusson were woven in tapestry, following the baroque and rococo elegance with their distinctive colours and opulent patterns combining fruits and the classic spiny acanthus leaves with floral garlands or medallions. Their appeal lies very much in this clarity of shades – the dusky pink, powder blue and velvety brown – all set on a neutral background. The flat-weave construction makes them very different from the more common knotted Savonneries. The Savonnerie was set up as a royal workshop in 1627 and continued to produce carpets for the court and state only. Typical designs were scrolls and acanthus leaves at the time of Louis XIV, flowing leaves and floral swags during the reign of Louis XV, and in Louis XVI's time a more classical style, often including the fleur-de-lis and the Napoleonic bee.

Turkish rugs, which appeared in France in the early 17th century, were kept at bay at the time to encourage internal trade. It is only in more recent years that the relatively low price and wide availability of these and other oriental rugs has meant an increase in their popularity in France as in the rest of Europe.

Natural floor coverings like sisal and coir are also increasing in demand, either used as mats or laid wall to wall. The French fully appreciate textiles as art forms and it is as usual to see a rug displayed on the wall, as a sofa throw or table cover, as it is on the floor. You might take inspiration for accessorizing from further back in French history when in the 19th century decorative hangings were used over doors, primarily as draught exclusion but making a colourful feature in the process. Many of these, made at Aubusson, had large hanging baskets of flowers and scrolling wreaths on dusky pink.

With the wealth of colourful rugs and unusual textiles at our disposal today creating a feature is easy. So for maximum impact in a living room, forget the muted tones and go for colour in a big way. Stay classic with fabrics, mix furniture styles and eras, add a mirror, pile on textures galore but above all do not be afraid to be bold. The result is French style at its most natural.

The influence of Thonet, who developed the bentwood chair, is seen throughout France, and indeed the world, not only in restaurants and hotels but also in the home. The appeal of the fluid lines of his pieces coupled with comfort have contributed to the perpetual popularity of the style. Just below the window you can just spot another classic textile – tapestry used as upholstery on an armchair. This, together with the mirrors and a collection of old glass decanters, makes this room clearly identifiable as French.

DOUBLE CURTAIN DRAPERY

In the early 19th century, double curtains, where a heavy silk brocade curtain was draped over an inner one of lightweight muslin, were a common feature. This idea of 'dress' curtains has remained popular and is perfect on a window that is not overlooked. Make up a functional sheer curtain (muslin makes a cheap option although it will eventually look grey and limp) and make a feature of the heavier drapes. Originally they would have been hung from splendid poles and decked with heavy fringing but a more sympathetic treatment for most homes today would be to forget the fringing and splash out on a stunning pole instead. There are many grand versions that are reminiscent of this look. Double metal rails designed to be used for curtains plus pelmet are a cheaper way of hanging two layers at once but avoid plastic – the plastic pelmet rail will not take the weight.

You will need

- Reversible fabric, either plain or damask
- Ready-made floor-length sheers

- 2 tie-back supports (door knobs will substitute)
- Needle and strong thread
- 2 bulldog clips

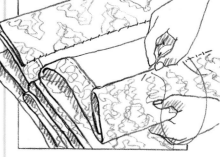

1 *To calculate the amount of fabric required, measure the drop, add on 25cm (10in) for top and hems, and multiply by the width of the fabric. Then multiply this figure by 2½ times the width of the window. Hang the sheer fabric from the curtain rail close to the glass.*

2 *Neaten the selvedges of the main fabric by turning under a 12mm (1½in) hem. Turn under double hems of 7.5cm (3in) at the top and bottom.*

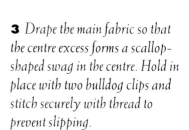

3 *Drape the main fabric so that the centre excess forms a scallop-shaped swag in the centre. Hold in place with two bulldog clips and stitch securely with thread to prevent slipping.*

4 *Fix tie-back supports at each side and drape fabric behind these to make elegant swags.*

CURTAIN TASSELS

Tassels have played a significant part in French interior design through the ages. Marie Antoinette was well documented for her tassel enthusiasm and in her palace, tassel-inspired designs were much in evidence, from wooden carvings and printed wallpapers to festoons on furnishings and window dressings. Today tassels still have their place and can make the simplest of window dressings look distinctive. Tassels can be made fairly simply but the whole effect relies on drape so it is worth investing in a quality yarn.

You will need
❋

- Skein of soft tubular yarn (velvet looks exceptionally sumptuous)
- Length of cord
- Strong thread in a complementary colour
- Fabric glue (optional)
- Scissors
- Large glass bead

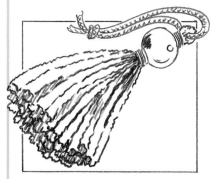

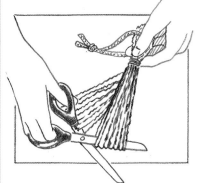

2 *Holding the skein by the corded end, carefully cut the loops at the bottom, taking care to stretch the yarn so that the lengths are the same.*

3 *Slip a large glass bead over the top of the skein and wind strong thread above the bead to fix it in place.*

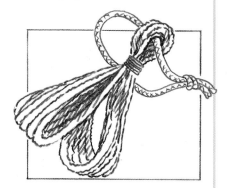

1 *Fold the skein of yarn in half. Tie the cord through the top loop. Wind thread around the skein, about 3cm (1¼in) down from the top, and secure the ends. (You may need to use glue too if the yarn is thick.)*

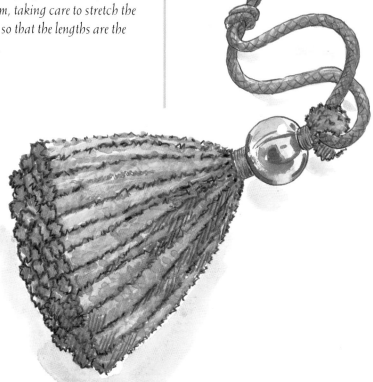

BOLSTER

Bolsters were a prominent feature of sofas in the Empire period and add a classic French feel to any living room. To reproduce the style closely they are best used with a low-armed sofa. The appropriate size of the bolster will depend on the depth of the sofa sides and length of the sofa. Small feather-filled bolsters are available from department stores; firmer foam-filled versions can be ordered. Foam dealers often trade from market stalls and will make a bolster to the required size. The ends of orginal bolsters were made from a separate piece of pleated material with a central rosette or tassel, but a similar effect can be achieved simply with one piece of fabric.

You will need

- Bolster cushion
- Fabric
- 2 large buttons that can be covered. Size should be in proportion to bolster.
- Needle
- Strong thread

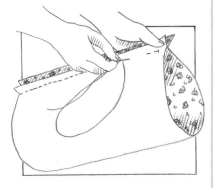

1 *Work out the quantity of fabric required by measuring the bolster length plus the diameter of the cross section and adding 3cm (1¼in) for seam allowances. Fold the fabric along the long edge with right sides together. Stitch along the raw edges, 1.5cm (⅝in) in from the edge.*

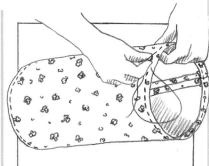

2 *Turn the fabric right side out. Turn under a 1.5cm (⅝in) at each end and stitch.*

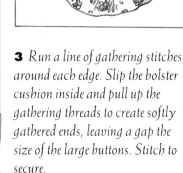

3 *Run a line of gathering stitches around each edge. Slip the bolster cushion inside and pull up the gathering threads to create softly gathered ends, leaving a gap the size of the large buttons. Stitch to secure.*

4 *Cover the buttons with matching fabric. Wrap the fabric over the top of the button, and gather it on the underside. Secure with a few stitches. Attach one button to each end of the bolster with a few stitches to secure.*

CHAPTER FIVE

Kitchens

THE DAY STARTS IN THE KITCHEN WITH A CROISSANT dunked in coffee and ends here with a tot of Calvados or another café noir. The kitchen is the hub of home life and it is appropriate that the product and the place where it all happens share the same name – *la cuisine*. Cooking and the kitchen are one and the same in France and you need to be an ardent foodie as well as a Francophile to get the most out of a French-style kitchen. French kitchens are more than meal preparation areas. They are social centres and business centres rolled into one and this business is extremely serious.

WORK AREA

Whether the kitchen is unfitted or fitted wall-to-wall with units, the emphasis should be on efficiency. Decor panels and the latest laminates should come way down the list of priorities. Rate higher a

1 *Ceramic floor*
2 *Sizeable table caters for extended family and friends*
3 *Freestanding dresser provides essential storage for local pottery*
4 *Pretty lace edging on shelves*
5 *Mismatched chairs*

6 *A traditional stove copes with cooking in quantity*
7 *Tablecloth made from a French country fabric*
8 *Bowls and pitchers are generous in size*

64

Opposite: A cool kitchen in a farmhouse cellar in rural Quercy is kept deliberately light and airy with white walls and simple furnishings. Typical French elements include the metal café-style chairs, wirework bottle carrier on the side table and capacious salt glaze pots and bowls. The stove-style cooker with double oven is the standard appliance.

Below: These mesh-fronted cupboards are modern variations on a theme of traditional food storage, much practised in France to keep cheese cool and fresh. The distressed paint finish adds a certain authenticity.

sizeable stove, practical work surface and ample shelves. The evidence of cooking should rarely be shut behind closed doors, and clear worktops are unusual. Do not put your pans away. Instead, hang them close to hand with the string of garlic and bunch of fresh herbs. Store fruit and vegetables in generous bowls and giant baskets.

CERAMICS

Pottery features largely in more ways than one in French kitchens. Faïence – earthenware pottery with an opaque glaze – is a popular choice. Designs are specific to each region although some families may have accumulated styles from various parts. Quimperware from West Brittany is among the most distinctive, with its cheerful hand-painted designs on an off-white background. It is the free brushstrokes that gives it its appeal, the most recognizable style carrying the little Breton figures or rooster.

Rustic pieces are as impressive for their scale as for colour. Use capacious pitchers in place of dainty jugs, chunky gratin dishes and casseroles instead of delicate bowls. Likewise, use breakfast cups the size of soup bowls in place of tiny tea cups.

FURNISHINGS

It is almost essential not to have a complete set of chairs around the kitchen table to reproduce French style, especially country, at its most natural state. Chairs are inevitably acquired from different branches of the family over the years and added to without worrying about matching types.

The table itself should be large to accommodate family and friends. In a French home, it is not uncommon to regularly seat three generations together at one meal. A farmhouse table is ideal for a country home. Provençal tables are traditionally chunky in style, long and rectangular in shape and can seat 12 in comfort. In town residences, neater bistro or café-style furniture fits the bill and bentwood is a popular choice.

Serious cooking demands serious appliances and a stove is

inevitably more suited to the French lifestyle than a standard-sized oven and hob. Many French homes have larger high-powered stoves that look something like a cross between an old-fashioned range and a professional stove. The latest models have added sophistications like multi-fuel power and griddle plates.

Old-fashioned butlers' sinks are widely used in French

Above: A sizeable stove is an essential in the French working kitchen. The well-used butcher's block that has absorbed the odours of French cuisine over the years – from chopping and herb crushing – adds character to the room. The soft blue painted units, wicker baskets and blonde wood work surface softens what could otherwise become a clinical environment with its vast expanse of ceramic tiles on walls and floor. Opposite: This metal baker's rack is a convincing copy of those used in the boulangerie for racking and stacking crusty French bread, and makes the perfect freestanding French-style kitchen storage.

kitchens. These are rectangular trough-shaped sinks made of fireclay, left plain or glazed white. Copies of early versions follow the basic design but they are glazed with vitreous enamel for resilience. Double sinks are considered sensible – one sink with soap suds to wash the dishes, another filled with plain water, changed regularly, to rinse soap suds off.

FLOOR

Floors in French-style kitchens should be tiled; an ideal choice would be tiles in simple terracotta made from low-fired red clay and left unglazed. Their characteristic variation in colour is due to the position in the kiln during firing and this irregularity is accepted in France as part of their charm. Tiles come in all shapes and sizes, although hexagons are typical of the south of France. It is fairly easy to source reclaimed French tiles from all over the country, including pale pinks from Provence and deep reds from Burgundy.

WALLS

Walls are for storage and as such their decoration should be underplayed. Choose a plain wash of white or earthy colours which complement the natural textures like terracotta and wood.

Interior walls in some areas of rural France where limestone rock is prevalent, like the Dordogne, Pyrenees, Cevennes, Juras and Provence, would at one time have been limewashed. It was recognized that this mix of slaked lime, water mixed with tallow (animal fat) or fig juice, was a good cover for these old walls because it allowed them to breathe and moisture could escape from the damp walls by evaporating from the surface. The walls in a cottage kitchen in these areas would be likely to have this distinctive chalky matt finish, either in natural white or coloured with local pigments

Opposite: An instant flavour of France is introduced into this English kitchen with a mid-19th century French cast iron and marble butcher's table, olive pots and a collection of early Quimper china from Brittany.

of earth colours like raw sienna, burnt umber and red and yellow ochre. The effect is characteristically uneven because of the tendency to absorb and release dampness. This in itself gives a delightful weathered look which is the perfect partner to old properties. Traditional limewash is still available but tricky and even dangerous to carry out. Modern day colourwashes in Mediterranean hues are a more convenient way of achieving a similar effect. Simply brush it roughly on to the surface in all directions so the brushmarks remain visible.

THE BUTCHER AND BAKER

Freestanding fittings are common for storage and food preparation in a French-style kitchen. Apart from the conventional butcher's block, marble-topped tables and baker's racks are handy for storage. The iron-slatted shelves of the baker's rack look appealing even when full to overflowing. Haphazard storage reiterates that the owner is a busy cook and what is stored is more important than how it is arranged.

French kitchens are not always planned to make a design statement. They are functional first and foremost although they could not be further from looking clinical. The miscellany of textures and colour comes together naturally from a mixture of the pottery – vivid acid-coloured glazes of salt glaze pots offset by the mellow terracotta; the cheerful yellows and blues of faïence or enamelware complimented by gleaming metal of copper pans; gunmetal grey of iron implements harmonizing with clay floor tiles. Added to this, though, is the French flair for detail, like prettying up raw timber shelves with crunchy lace edging or a crisp embroidered trim, or just throwing a tablecloth over the table or hanging a simple curtain made from a fresh cotton print. Practical by deliberation they are, pretty sometimes by accident they may be, but the fact that French kitchens are comfortable to live in, makes them appealing and one of the most popular kitchen styles to be emulated, albeit often inaccurately, by foreigners.

$\mathcal{P}$ROJECTS

EMBROIDERED SHELF TRIM

Embroidered edgings are a favourite way of finishing off a shelf in French country kitchens. Lengths of ready-embroidered fabric are available by the metre in France for this purpose but it is fun to make an original from scratch.

You will need

- Tracing paper
- Pencil
- Pins
- Linen

- Scissors
- Iron
- Matching sewing thread
- Skein of embroidery thread

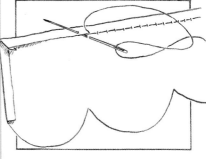

2 *Press under the allowance shown along the top long edge and two short sides and hem to neaten, either by hand or machine.*

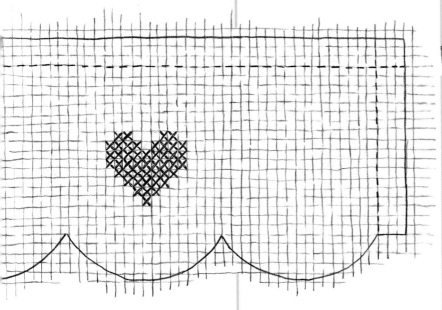

1 *Copy the design (shown half-size above) onto tracing paper and pin this to the length of linen, which is 14cm (5½in) deep x length of shelf plus 3cm (1⅝in). Carefully cut out the linen shape, following the outline of the tracing paper.*

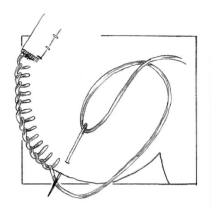

3 *Neaten the scalloped edge either by hand using loop stitch as shown, or by zigzag machine stitching.*

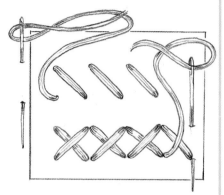

4 *Using coloured embroidery thread, embroider cross stitch hearts centrally on each alternate scallop. To do this, bring the needle up at the bottom right corner of the square. Take it diagonally across the square and down at the top left corner. To complete the cross, bring the needle up at the bottom left corner and down again at the top right corner. Stitch all crosses in the same way.*

COLOURWASHED WALLS

Softly washed walls are reminiscent of interiors in the south of France. This soft washed effect gives depth of tone and is best done in earthy colours like terracotta and sun-bleached ochre. To maximize this impression of depth, build up three tonal layers starting with the darker shade first. There is no point in lining walls when you are intending to tackle this paint effect. Do not worry about filling holes in the plaster. Defects and irregularities add to the rustic charm of the finish.

You will need

- Emulsion paint
- Water
- Decorator's brush

1 *Before you begin, your wall should have a white or light-coloured background. Dilute the emulsion paint in the proportion of 3 parts water to 1 part paint. Dip a brush in the colourwash and apply paint randomly on the wall,* pulling the brush in every direction so that you make irregular brushmarks.

2 *Continue to brush quickly over the whole surface with a damp brush to blend and soften the brushmarks. Dilute the colourwash even more, then repeat. The final effect has the impression of a roughly painted wall.*

$\mathcal{B}$EDROOMS

THE RESTFUL BEDROOM WE LOVE TODAY has to be credited to the rococo era in France and, most specifically, to Madame Pompadour, Louis XV's outgoing mistress. Her passion for delicate pastel hues filtered through all aspects of interior design at the time including Aubusson tapestry, and it was she who first brought shades we now call powder pink and pompadour blue to furnishings and walls – colours that have been greatly favoured in the bedroom ever since. But Madame de Pompadour is not the only Frenchwoman to step out of her bed on to an Aubusson rug. These delightful carpets are still appreciated today by the French and other enthusiastic homemakers alike and reproductions are widely available. Their exquisite designs of floral and fruit garlands coupled with the soft colourings have ensured that these tapestry floor coverings dating back to the 18th century reign on.

The bedroom is one of the few rooms of the house where the French are likely to lay a fitted carpet although bare floorboards,

1 *Classic French bed in rich timber*
2 *Cotton bedspread*
3 *Bare wooden floorboards*
4 *Broderie-edged sheer curtains*

5 *A corner devoted to grooming*
6 *A spot reserved for writing*
7 *Soft colouring reigns – butterscotch walls teamed with natural white*

Opposite: Madame de Pompadour was the inspiration for soft colours like rose pink in the bedroom. Painting walls and woodwork in gentle pastel tones or with natural hints are the perfect route to this delicate effect. A traditional-style bed piled with white embroidered linen carries through the French style into the furnishings.

usully topped with a rug, are still much more common than in other countries. Tradition is the backbone of the French bedroom. To most French folk, the thought of throwing away the old and bringing in the new is unheard of. Beds are particularly precious and some couples sleep in the same bed, not only as their parents before them but their grandparents, too.

Some beds in French homes were certainly built to stay – and have done so surviving three centuries and proving wholeheartedly that the fitted bedroom is far from a new concept. Beds literally boxed into panelling like this exist in parts of Brittany, usually in tiny one- or two-roomed cottages. The wooden surrounds can be carved or painted; some are complete with sliding doors for privacy and keeping out draughts; others are open and would have been draped. Two extra thick straw-filled mattresses would have been used for each of these beds, reaching such heights they resembled the image conjured up by the fairytale 'The Princess and the Pea'. A modified version of a box bed like this makes a perfect bed-cum-den for a child's room today with scope for inventive make-believe games and practical storage.

For those who love traditional styling but who need or prefer to buy new, contemporary manufacturers are constantly drawing on past styles for inspiration and there is an ever increasing choice of convincing reproductions available.

At its most rustic, the French bedroom is charming, and at its most refined, luxurious, but whichever style, it is always inviting in an extraordinarily simple way.

BEDS

In aristocratic circles, beds have always been equated with status in France. Louis XIV's bed was said to be equivalent to his throne and was decorated with tassel trimmings on the four posts as well as carved wooden tassels.

But not all French beds are so elaborate. In recent years, more sedate French bed styles of the 18th and 19th centuries have gained popularity way beyond the country's borders. It is their elegance

coupled with the sheer beauty of the typical fruitwood that makes
them so desirable. The specific bed shape depends on the era, but
they all share a certain fluidity of form.

Original beds may have sentimental overtones but in many
ways are not practical. Reproductions have been modified to retain
the favourable characteristics and drop the bad points. Old beds
may look wonderful but were small and inevitably uncomfortable.
An old bed often means a non-standard sized bed, which in turn
leads to having a custom-made mattress – an expensive route.
Interpretations of old beds for a new market generally mean that
they are not as heavy or cumbersome and options of painted
versions or light woods like beech make them more appropriate for
modern-day bedrooms.

The favourite styles are the Empire – a light bed with a flipped-

This bedroom, a farmhouse hayloft in the Tarn region of southern France, typifies a French rural bedroom with its bare floor, rough wall and basic bâteau lit. The objects scattered on the wall look perfectly appropriate in this country setting and make a fascinating feature and composition of shape and form.

over post; Louis Phillipe-style boat or sleigh bed with a scroll head and foot end that originated in the mid-19th century and took its name from the pronounced S-shape resembling a boat; and the Directoire with a straight head and foot end and a flip-over top. For a comprehensive choice of reproductions it is worth visiting a specialist bed shop. However, national high street chain stores are now producing their own brands and this has widened the availability of these French classics.

Earlier beds were so excessive in their dressing that it is almost impossible to identify with them as a feasible source of inspiration for bedrooms today. Modifications are usually more appropriate and the best short cut to a French-style draped bed is positioning the bed so that its side runs against the wall and then taking drapes from the back wall. There are all sorts of devices available in soft furnishing departments that make draping straightforward to do in any bedroom.

This ploy of adapting a French style to suit your home will give your home originality. In the 17th century, on the one extreme in poorer households were the boxed beds, while society people slept in beds that were decorated to the hilt with integral carvings, finials and hangings.

For older girls or even adults, a romantic bed like the elaborate 18th-century Lit à la Polonnaise is the style to copy. With its extravagant swags of fabric from a central corona looking something like an Austrian blind, it is the ultimate in extravagant draped beds.

BED LINEN

You can tell a great deal about bed linen by driving around France mid-morning when the bedcovers are inevitably draped out of the window or over balconies for an airing. The duvet was called the continental quilt because Europeans were using it way before the British. The decorative duvet cover as we know it is a relatively recent phenomenon and even now is not used universally in France. The quilt is as likely to be enclosed in a cover made of plain white sheeting with a counterpane or bedspread thrown over the top, as on its own as a top cover with a sheet underneath. Originally the bedspread would have been of white ribbed cotton and used together with a blanket – the name itself stems from the French word blankete which was derived from blanc, also white. Long bolster-like pillows supported conventional ones – an arrangement that remains unchanged today with pillows on top, square as opposed to rectangular.

Despite the convenience of easy-care fabrics, the French on the whole are still devotees of natural fibres. Their use goes far back in French history. Pure linen itself was preferred for sheets by wealthier folk, although sheets made from the coarser fibres like hemp were used for those with less money. All sheets were made up with seams. (This applied right up until the 1930s) and in the 17th century sheets and pillowcases were trimmed with Flemish lace. So, for a French-style bedroom, choose linen, cotton and lace.

Decorated linen was highly fashionable and adornment could be white embroidered on the white background, openwork embroidery or lace inserts. At the time of the second Empire around the 1860s the look became more feminine, with finer lawn fabrics, delicate lace inserts and embroidered muslin featuring prominently in bed linen.

This practice of hand trimming bed linen came naturally to the French who learned the skill of embroidery at school throughout the 19th and in the earlier part of the 20th century. Decorated linen was a standard item in the home, often made by the lady of the household herself. Over the years skills faded, and more practical ready-made versions of bed linen have become readily available at reasonable prices. Torchon lace, a strong bobbin lace made with flax thread, was once the main contender for trimming bed linen because of its resilience and low price, but as inexpensive machine-made lace from the Far East has been used to decorate commercial bed linen, hand-made practices have dwindled.

WINDOWS

Lace or sheer fabrics screen most bedroom windows in France. They are either stretched on brass rods or wires close to the glass or hang freely from slender rails making functional curtains that can be drawn. This use of sheer fabrics provides privacy at the same time as filtering light. The draping quality adds an ethereal feel to any bedroom and introduces softness even in a room where bare boards could otherwise create a cold, even monastic atmosphere.

Early versions of window sheers include muslin as well as linens and lace hand-made locally in cotton. Some of these handmade works of art are still used, especially in rural villages in uncommercialized areas like Brittany where you can still spot originals like *Broderie des Indes* – muslin with drawn threadwork named after the Indian cotton scarves of a similar style that were imported from India in the 18th century. Embroidered net curtains are sometimes seen although they are rarer as their delicate nature makes them prone to rotting. Sunlight is the greatest enemy of textiles; it bleaches them, which eventually leads to the threads deteriorating and rotting. Coarse bobbin lace, like Cluny, is tougher and was used to make popular screens that have survived the years and are still made in some areas today. However, their dense patterns mean they are not the best choice to allow light through, making them more decorative than functional. These days, the majority of bedroom windows tend to be dressed with finer machine-made Raschel lace in a variety of patterns; this has become used widely not least because of its practical machine-washable qualities.

Floor-length lace panels are the easiest route to an elegant French style bedroom but to echo the French preferences opt for a

simple pattern in the weave; heavy Victorian-style florals should be avoided. For cheap window dressing, use muslin in generous quantitites although it will eventually yellow and look limp.

FURNITURE

The old faithful armoire makes an appearance again in the bedroom where it is used for its traditional purpose of housing linen. At one time an armoire would have been given as a wedding gift complete with stacks of essential sheets and bedspreads. Chunky chests of drawers provide valuable storage space, too, inevitably topped with a batch of perfume bottles of all shapes and sizes in quantities akin to a perfumerie section in a department store. The French take their fragrances seriously, frequently possessing a selection of eau de toilettes and perfumes so that they can vary their scent to suit their mood. It is not unusual to see a collection of antique bottles in a French bedroom. Some of these are exceptionally beautiful, like those of Jean Despres from the end of the 18th century with white porcelain cameo heads set into crystal glass. Stunning too are Lalique's moulded and etched creations containing the perfumes of Coty, Worth, Houbigant, Roger et Gallet and Nina Ricci; although mass produced, they have the appearance of hand-made glass.

For centuries, bedroom drawers have been perfumed with fragrant silk sachets filled with a cotton padding soaked in perfume. Alternatively, lavender, so abundant in the south of France, was used to fill the sachet. Bunches of lavender or just flower petals were also hung in cupboards.

The bedroom, although primarily a room for dressing and relaxing, is used as much for retiring to write a diary or letters in the afternoon as it is for sleeping. A typical French bedroom is quite likely to include a writing table, making this room yet another one in the French household that serves several purposes.

The French bedroom at the end of the day is elegant and pretty but as practical as any other room in the house. At its most rustic it is charming and at its most refined, luxurious, but whichever style, it is always inviting in an extraordinarily simple way.

$\mathscr{P}$ROJECTS

POT POURRI

Pot pourri has its origins in 18th-century France. Literally translated it means 'rotten pot' and refers to the aromatic plants which were literally left to rot and dry then preserved in a pot to scent the air. These days it is easier to make a dry pot pourri. There are hundreds of recipes for different fragrances but this one is made up from common summer garden flowers and compiled as much for its colour as its perfume. Pile the mixture into the largest bowl you can find and create a visual as well as aromatic pleasure in the bedroom

You will need

❈

- Brightly coloured garden flowers, such as delphiniums, cornflowers, roses, pansies and calendula
- String
- Large plastic-lidded food container
- Silica gel (available from chemists)
- Draining spoon

- Artist's paintbrush
- 1 tablespoon orris root powder
- 1 teaspoon ground cloves
- 1 teaspoon ground nutmeg
- 1 teaspoon ground cinnamon
- Pot pourri oil
- Clingfilm

1 *Gather a bunch of fresh garden flowers. This is best done on a second dry, sunny day at mid-morning, just after the dew has dried. Collect the different varieties over the whole flowering season and make the pot pourri mixture when autumn approaches and you can no longer enjoy them fresh.*

2 *With each bunch, reserve a few flowerheads to dry in silica gel (by this method flowers remain almost perfect in form and colour so are ideal for the top of the pot pourri). Dry the rest of the flowers by tying in bunches and hanging in a cool dry place where air can circulate around them. This takes about one week.*

continued over ➤

3 To silica-dry flowers, fill a plastic box about one third full with silica gel. Place the flowers on the gel facing upwards (if they are flat-petalled like daisies, face them downwards). Press them gently into the gel until the entire flower is covered. Do not be tempted to pour gel on top or to pack too many flowers in as it will crush the blooms. Replace the lid and check daily until the flowers are dry but not crisp and brittle (this usually takes from three to seven days, depending on the type of flower). Remove the flowers gently with a draining spoon and store them flat until you are ready to make the pot pourri mixture. Brush away any remaining gel with a soft artist's paintbrush.

4 Mix the flowerheads that have been hang-dried together in a large bowl.

5 Add orris root powder and the mixed spices and toss gently. Add a few drops of pot pourri oil, mixing well.

6 Seal the bowl with clingfilm and leave the mixture for six weeks for the pot pourri to mature.

7 Add silica-dried flowers to the mixture and use it to fill a decorative bowl in the bedroom. Refresh the pot pourri periodically with pot pourri oil.

DRAPED BED

Anyone might question the practicality of a heavily draped bed, especially one as elaborate as the state bed of King Louis XIV in the Palace of Versailles, which had so many swathes of fabrics and trimmings that it was difficult to identify what lay beneath. Bolsters and brocaded bedcovers complete with braids and trimmings are just too much work. Duvets, once a phenomenon of Europe, have gained popularity everywhere because of their ease of use. But soft cascades of fabric from a canopy is a compromise. It has a romanticism that is appealing and it is easy to reconstruct the look. It is not difficult to adapt an elegant look inspired by the Napoleonic era and, with the right accessories, the fabric need not get in the way.

You will need

- Drape ring or curtain pole and 2 tie-back hooks
- Screwdriver
- Soft fabric
- Heading tape
- Matching thread
- Curtain hooks

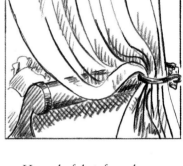

3 *Hang the fabric from the curtain pole using curtain hooks and drape it around the bed, looping it around the tie-back hooks.*

2 *Work out the length of fabric you will need — it will depend on the height of your bed and the height of your ceiling. Hem the two pieces of fabric and attach heading tape to the top side.*

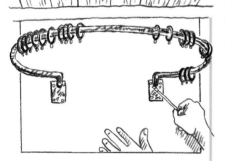

1 *On a double bed construct the canopy at the head; on a single bed consider pushing the bed with its side against the wall. Check out the latest kits and draping aids in department stores or simply screw a curtain pole to the ceiling and two hooks against the wall on either side of the pole adjacent with the bed.*

CHAPTER SEVEN

Bathrooms

ROMANTICS AT HEART WILL ADORE a French bathroom, especially an old French bath. Traditional-style tubs were made for two, designed with the taps at the centre and a place to lean at either end for a soak. The disadvantage was that they were much shorter in length than the baths we are used to today so that bathing *à deux* was far from a comfortable operation.

But, as for looks, you cannot beat the double-ended bath; teamed with a shapely fluted basin, shower and floaty sheer curtains, it creates a French style inspired by the turn of the century – a bathroom made of dreams. It is not impossible to recreate this reflective mood today – enterprising retailers are making certain that such quality fittings are not forgotten, while manufacturers are turning out adaptations of authentic styles.

For a practical interpretation, mix originals with present-day

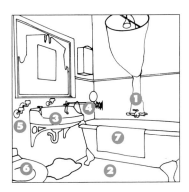

1 *Original Jacob Delafon nickel-plated globe shower mixer/riser*
2 *Wooden floor*
3 *Simple French D-shape basin on clasp brackets mixed with English Victorian Dhali taps*
4 *French triple-pronged towel rail*

5 *French pierced nickel-plated cupholders*
6 *French toilet manufactured in England*
7 *French embroidered table linen used as a bath mat*

Opposite: This efficiently organized bathroom reflects the French attitude that function comes first and foremost. With a double sink and two flexible mirrors plus two on the wall, all prominently placed, la toilette can be carried out to perfection.

conveniences, but avoid the rubber bathmat and replace with a cotton woven variety instead.

Current-day bathrooms in France are not a million miles away from suites elsewhere in the world. To recreate French style at its best, look to the past. The bathroom as such made its debut thanks to Louis XVI who was the first Frenchman to have a bathroom installed. But it was not until the late 19th century, when running water was available on tap, that more homes started to have this new convenience.

Styles have changed little over the years and the French bathroom has captured the imagination of many. Some French bathrooms, though, appear to be severe for our luxurious tastes and the decor may need careful treatment. After the French Revolution, French interiors were transformed throughout the country with the decorative being replaced by the functional. This, plus the fact that the French consider *la toilette* a serious daily ritual, accounts for extremely efficiently planned bathrooms, which in some cases are so structured that they may seem institutional. The regular black and white tiled floor adds to this and such a room will need compensating with lashings of sheer fabric, sympathetic-coloured paintwork and stacks of soft towels to restore the balance. Twin basins are part of this move towards a functional environment and are a fairly common find, either as one purpose-built unit or two identical pedestals fitted as a pair.

BATHS

Some of the original French bathroom fittings are so stunning that they have become cherished and as fast as they are being removed from hotels, chateaux or even hospitals, they are being snapped up by salvage enthusiasts, reconditioned and reinstated back in homes where they can be enjoyed. The most well-known type of French bath is made from copper. Naturally occuring in the south of France, copper was an obvious choice of material and looks appealing with its brushed pink hue.

These baths look particularly impressive when placed centrally

A high-sided copper bath with its characteristic pink hue makes this quaint bathroom positively glow. A compact marble-topped vanity unit is particularly neat , providing useful storage in this tight area, while mirrors on four walls give a much-needed illusion of space.

in a room, fitted with polished brass taps or aligned to a wall with a high-mounted shower riser and crowned with a circular hoop. A regular bath style was the oval-shaped Cleopatra; the slipper was tapered at one end and the chariot shaped like the vessel it was named after. It was common practice to use a copper liner inside another bath to guard against leaks.

The cast iron bath, porcelain-enamelled with a wide flange edge, was the norm in the majority of French houses. Between 1870 and 1920 there were many different sizes and shapes. Feet varied in style from traditional ball and claw to scroll, columns, florals, acanthus leaves and gothic arches.

Marble baths were less common. Extremely ornate in design, these were often based on classical designs with ornamental legs modelled on bestial imagery and featuring devils, serpents, or lions' feet. French porcelain basins are particularly popular, basically because they are so pretty, and for this reason the styles have been widely reproduced. Their shape is on the whole much simpler and chunkier than the English equivalent, with the pedestals fluted like a column and flared out at the base. A proportion of the French sanitary-ware dating from the late 19th century was in fact made in Britain. The French excelled in bathroom accessories and most of the elegant bathroom fittings like soap dishes, towel rails and robe hooks are French in origin.

Vanity units are also favoured in France, with many being custom-built and basins fitted into old cupboards or adapted with marble surrounds.

LINEN

Linen and lace were both used to great effect in the bathroom, with lengths featured decoratively on any piece of furniture. Bath linen was commonly decorated with Point d'Angleterre embroidery, decked with embroidered floral bouquets or trimmed with Alençon lace made in Normandy; this classic design at its most intricate included architecturally arranged flowers and swags worked into the pattern, while at its simplest it was a design made up of dots. Old linen can sometimes be picked up from house clearances and street markets, and is worth investing in for its decorative value.

As in the bedroom, windows should be screened by sheer fabrics and mirrors play an important functional role.

FLOORING

Flooring is inevitably tiled, partly because of practicalities of hygiene, but mostly because ceramics are so widely available in France and hence inexpensive. They are also are a sensible option, being cool underfoot in summer – a boon in warmer regions. In Provence, the floor is almost certain to be of terracotta tiles, either

Continental-style ceramic floors are undoubtedly a practical flooring especially in the bathroom, but can be in danger of becoming too clinical. The little touches like the lace edging on the shelf and the sheer fabric stretched across the screen go a long way in counteracting this. Paint has been cleverly used to give dimension and atmosphere to this bathroom by creating a false dado with a painted band, and vertical stripes added above.

Practices of the past have always inspired French designers and Phillipe Starck is no exception. This contemporary bathroom includes a bath based on an old-fashioned washtub, and a basin modelled on a bucket.

matt or glazed in a variety of shapes and sizes from large squares to the characteristic hexagons. In other areas, black and white tiles are standard, although in more exclusive homes, marble tiles are sometimes found.

Bathroom design has come full circle. Having passed through a phase of the fitted suite, the mixing of unique pieces is now here to stay and traditional French styles, whether real or copies, are much in demand. A recent bathroom innovation from one of the most famous contemporary French designers is an interesting move in this same direction. The latest design to come out of Phillipe Starck's studio is modelled on the most primitive of bathrooms, the tap based on a village pump, the toilet shape derived from a bucket, and the bath reminiscent of a genuine wooden barrel tub. It looks surprisingly elegant!

$\mathcal{P}$ROJECTS

LACE-TRIMMED TOWEL

Terry towels, as we know them, are a late 19th-century inspiration. Before this, towels were made from linen and the best ones were monogrammed and decorated with lace inserts, openwork, fringes or Richelieu work – embroidery with the appearance of lace. You can arrive at a compromise between the charm of old lace and the high absorbency of the new looped towels quite easily by trimming some of your own.

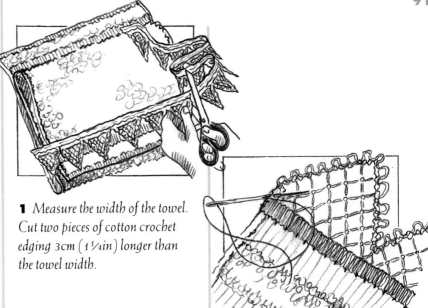

You will need

*

- Tape measure
- White towel
- Scissors
- Antique cotton crochet edging
- Needle
- Strong sewing thread

1 *Measure the width of the towel. Cut two pieces of cotton crochet edging 3cm (1¼in) longer than the towel width.*

2 *Turn under the raw edges of the crochet edging and oversew firmly to the towel using strong sewing thread.*

SWEET BAGS

Throughout French history, sweet bags have been tucked among linens or tied to chairbacks and bedposts to perfume rooms. Louis XIV loved scented sheets, his favourite fragrances being nutmeg, cloves, storax and benzoin boiled in rose water and combined with orange flowers, jasmine and a little musk. Marie Antoinette preferred the natural fragrance of roses and violets. Napoleon favoured rosemary, thyme and cloves while Josephine adored musk. Originally made from taffeta and silk, sachets were filled with cotton stuffing that had been saturated in perfume and tucked among the bath and bed linen in the linen cupboard or hung between the shelves. Sweet bags were made using the same basic herbs as pot pourri but the proportions were different; the perfume enclosed in the fabric of the sweet bags was more pungent.

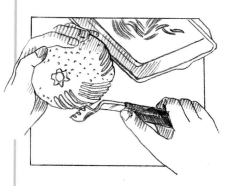

2 *Use a zester or fine potato peeler to remove fragments of peel of a large orange. Lay them on a baking tray, sprinkle with orris root powder and dry in an oven at 100°F/50°C. Mix together the lavender, rosemary and dried orange peel. Take a handful of this mixture and mix with the cloves.*

You will need
❋

- Small bunch of lavender flowers
- Small bunch of rosemary
- Zester or potato peeler
- 1 orange
- Baking tray
- Orris root powder
- 12 whole cloves
- 18 x 15cm (7¼ x 6in) muslin or other fine-woven cotton fabric
- Sewing thread
- Sewing machine
- 27 x 14.5cm (10¾ x 5¾in) fine white cotton/linen fabric
- 30cm (12in) narrow lace trimming
- 50cm (20in) narrow ribbon

1 *Prepare the fragrant filling. Gather lavender and rosemary. These are best picked on a second dry, sunny day at mid-morning after the dew has dried. Some lavenders are less fragrant than others but for maximum scent gather when the buds have reached the deep purple but not quite open stage. Hang the bunch upside down to dry. This can take a week depending on the weather. Remove leaves and seeds when dry.*

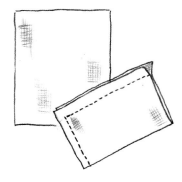

3 *Make the inner muslin sachet. Fold the muslin in half along its length so the right sides are facing. Machine along one long side and one short side. Turn inside out.*

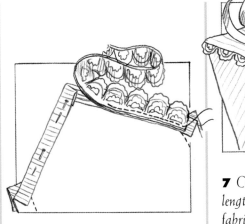

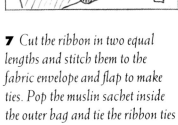

4 *Fill the sachet with fragrant filling, then machine along the top short edge to secure.*

6 *Turn under the two sides of the triangle shape to the wrong side and press. Machine stitch these edges in place, attaching the lace trimming at the same time. Turn the outer bag to the right side.*

7 *Cut the ribbon in two equal lengths and stitch them to the fabric envelope and flap to make ties. Pop the muslin sachet inside the outer bag and tie the ribbon ties to close.*

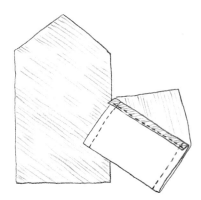

5 *Make up the outer bag. Cut out the fabric and fold as shown. Turn the long raw edge to the wrong side and press. Fold over the bottom long edge of the fabric to meet the top triangle. Machine stitch the two side seams, catching down the pressed edge.*

$\mathcal{I}$NDEX

ACKNOWLEDGEMENTS

Photographs courtesy of:
Flooring by Amtico Image Library 0800 667 766 p.43; Annet Held/Arcaid p.57; Laura
Ashley 0800 868 100 p.17; Camera Press/Appeltofft pp.12, 52; Manuel Canovas Ltd:
0171 225 2298 p.7; Crown Paint: 0171 494 1331 p.20; The Design Archives: 01202
762699 p.11; Dulux: 01753 550555 pp.75, 89; The Cluny 1052 by Fourneaux de
France: 0181 232 8882 p.66; Pierre Frey: 0171 376 5599 p.9; Meubles Grange (UK
Ltd): 01780 54721 pp.14, 32, 67; Simon Brown/Homes & Gardens/Robert Harding
Syndication p.69; Christopher Drake/Homes & Gardens/Robert Harding Syndication
p.40; Nadia Mackenzie/Country Homes & Interiors/Robert Harding Syndication
p.62–3; David Montgomery/Homes & Gardens/Robert Harding Syndication p.55;
Spike Powell/Homes & Gardens/Robert Harding Syndication p.76; Trevor
Richards/Homes & Gardens/Robert Harding Syndication pp.84–5; Paul RyanHomes &
Gardens/Robert Harding Syndication pp.50–1; Fritz von der Schulenburg/Country
Homes & Interiors/Robert Harding Syndication pp.31, 65; C.P.Hart: 0171 902 1000
p.90; caned lit bateau by Simon Horn Furniture: 0171 731 1279 p.79; James
Mortimer/The Interior Archives: 0171 370 0595 pp.35, 54, 88; Fritz von der
Schulenburg/The Interior Archives pp.27, 72–3, 87; Somerset Creative Products:
01278 641622 p.64; Rail Express extra track from Swish p.26; *Promenade des Anglais*
collection from Today Interiors Ltd p.41; Coté Ouest/Elizabeth Whiting & Associates
pp.19, 24, 38–9, 44; Coté Sud/Elizabeth Whiting & Associates pp.23, 28–9; Andreas
von Einsiedel/Elizabeth Whiting & Associates p.53; Dennis Stone/Elizabeth Whiting
& Associates p.30; Elizabeth Whiting & Associates p.25.

All paint effect materials and stencils available from branches of The Stencil Store,
20–21 Heronsgate Road, Chorleywood, Herts WD3 5BN. Tel: 01923 285 577, French
bathroom fittings available from The Water Monopoly, 16–18 Lonsdale Road, London
NW6 6RD. Tel: 0171 624 2636.

The author would like to thank:
Marion Jenkins, Patricia Newitt, Martin Long of The Carpet Library, Rosemary Green
of The Lace Guild, Michael Flinn of The Stencil Store, Jennie Emery, Jenny West,
Belinda Coote Tapestry, Samantha von Daniken of The Water Monopoly.